loop, print, fade + flicker:
David Rimmer's Moving Images

loop, print, fade + flicker:
David Rimmer's Moving Images

ESSAY BY MIKE HOOLBOOM

INTERVIEW BY ALEX MACKENZIE

PACIFIC CINÉMATHÈQUE MONOGRAPH SERIES
NUMBER ONE

24 per second
THE ANVIL FILM SERIES

Anvil Press Publishers Inc.
P.O. Box 3008, Main Post Office
Vancouver, B.C. V6B 3X5 CANADA
www.anvilpress.com

LIBRARY AND ARCHIVES CANADA CATALOGUING IN PUBLICATION

Hoolboom, Michael

    Loop, print, fade + flicker : David Rimmer's moving images / Mike Hoolboom.

(Pacific cinémathèque monograph series ; 1)
Includes bibliographical references and index.
ISBN 978-1-895636-98-7

    1. Rimmer, David, 1942-. 2. Experimental films--Canada.
I. Title. II. Title: Loop, print, fade and flicker. III. Series: Pacific cinematheque monograph series 1
PN1998.3.R55 H65 2009   791.4302'3092   C2009-900256-6

Printed and bound in Canada
Cover design: Mutasis Creative
Interior design: Heimat House
Anvil Film Series, *24 per second*, #1

Represented in Canada by the Literary Press Group
Distributed by the University of Toronto Press

Canadian Patrimoine
Heritage canadien

The publisher gratefully acknowledges the financial assistance of the Canada Council for the Arts, the Book Publishing Industry Development Program (BPIDP), and the Province of British Columbia through the B.C. Arts Council and the Book Publishing Tax Credit.

IMAGE PAGE 2: SQUARE INCH FIELD, 1968.

CONTENTS

Preface

THE PACIFIC CINÉMATHÈQUE MONOGRAPH SERIES

Western Canadian cinema has been and continues to be one of the most geographically and artistically expansive, distinctive, and dynamic zones, both within the cultural borders of Canada and within the cinematic traditions of North American cinema. Yet it also remains, with a few exceptions, one of the most under-analyzed and under-represented areas in both mainstream film studies and independent film criticism. The NFB documentary traditions that were forged in Ottawa, following on the heels of John Grierson and the post-1960s Québécois regional cinema led by Denys Arcand and Claude Jutra, have received their well-deserved critical dues. For too long now Western Canadian filmmaking practice has been simplistically categorized, to use the global vernacular, as a spin-off of "Hollywood North." A place for exploring and acknowledging the spectrum of contributions and innovations of Western Canadian filmmakers, videomakers, and fringe media artists is therefore long overdue.

The Pacific Cinémathèque Monograph Series emerged out of this somewhat shadowy status of Western Canadian cinema within the field of film studies in particular and in the world of film appreciation in general. The subject of this series is the wide range of film-, video- and media-makers that have made significant contributions to either

FACING PAGE: SEASHORE, 1971

defining, expanding, or subverting the boundaries of Western Canadian cinema—from fringe to mainstream and back again—over the last fifty years. The series is overseen by the Education Department of the Pacific Cinémathèque. It builds on the success of Pacific Cinémathèque's Film Study Guide Series, and expands the audience of these popular guides by targeting film- and video-makers, film aficionados, undergraduate university students, and educators.

Each volume of the series will address an individual film- or media-maker and will consists of four different sections:

(i)   A critical essay introduces the reader to the regional, sociological, and artistic influences of the filmmaker— establishing both a historical and an environmental context for their body of work.

(ii) An extensive interview provides a thorough examination of the themes and mechanics behind the narrative and stylistic sensibilities of the interviewee—providing an in-depth exploration of the unique traits of the artist.

(iii) A detailed filmography is included as a reference guide to the artist's body of work.

(iv) A working bibliography situates the films and the influence of the filmmakers in a network of references assembled from a variety of sources: encyclopedias of cinema, essays, books, journals, and magazines.

ABOUT THE PROJECT SUPPORTERS

PACIFIC CINÉMATHÈQUE

Vancouver's Pacific Cinémathèque Pacifique is a not-for-profit society dedicated to fostering an understanding of film and moving images. Since 1972, the Cinémathèque's theatre and Education Department have been providing media education resources and materials to public schools across Canada. Through exhibitions, film tours, educational services, and film-related resources, Pacific Cinémathèque fosters critical media literacy and advances cinema as an art and as a vital means of communication in British Columbia and Canada.

AV PRESERVATION TRUST & CANADIAN HERITAGE

For the first volumes of the Monograph series, Pacific Cinémathèque has partnered with the AV Preservation Trust of Canada. The AV Preservation Trust is a charitable non-profit organization dedicated to promoting the preservation of Canada's audio-visual heritage, and to facilitating access to and usage of regional and national collections through partnerships with members of the audio-visual community. It is dedicated to increasing Canadians' awareness of their rich and distinctive heritage in moving images and sound. Working in collaboration with both public and private sectors, the AV Trust conducts a variety of programs designed to help tomorrow's generations see and hear the work of yesterday's and today's audio-visual creators.

This project was also made possible by funding provided through the Heritage Policy Branch of the Department of Canadian Heritage.

Acknowledgements

While it is true that the first installments of the Monograph Project have only now arrived in their finished print state, the project as a whole has passed through the hands and the minds of many. The current caretakers of the series owe a great debt to a plurality of editors, supporters, and advisors who helped guide the development and execution of the project.

Appreciation goes out to the various dedicated hands and minds that made these volumes possible. Special appreciation and recognition for Liz Schulze, Education Manager, Pacific Cinémathèque; Sally Stubbs, former Education Director, Pacific Cinémathèque; Dr. Stuart Poyntz, former Education Director, Pacific Cinémathèque; Jim Sinclair, Executive Director, Pacific Cinémathèque; Analee Weinberger, former Education Director, Pacific Cinémathèque; Colin Browne, filmmaker, writer and Professor, Contemporary Arts, Simon Fraser University; Caroline Coutts, Festival Director, Moving Pictures: Canadian Films on Tour; Zoë Druick, Assistant Professor, School of Communication, Simon Fraser University; Kelly Friesen, AV Preservation Trust; Danielle Currie, Vancouver Art Gallery; Meghan Elie, Moving Images Distribution; Brian Kaufman, Anvil Press; Catherine Gloor, Capilano University, and Steve Chow, Communications Manager, Pacific Cinémathèque.

In addition, special thanks for a variety of contributions goes out to the following: Amber Rowell, Betty Lou Phillips, Jean Wilson at UBC Press, Natalie Clager, Josh Byer, and Al Razutis. Finally, it is important to acknowledge that throughout the development of this series the Pacific Cinémathèque has relied on the resources of the Toronto Film Reference Library, the Ontario Cinémathèque, and the Vancouver Art Gallery.

—Brian Ganter, Editor,
on behalf of the Pacific Cinémathèque Education Department
Vancouver, BC, January 2009

Introduction

The films of David Rimmer are ideal for opening up what we hope will be a long-running series on the most significant and influential works of mid-century and contemporary Western Canadian cinema. It was in 1967-68, around the time Rimmer became employed at the Vancouver branch of the Canadian Broadcasting Corporation as a negative cutter and film editor, that he made his first inroads into experimental cinema. Since then he has acceded to a place in the pantheon of Canadian independent filmmakers including Michael Snow, Joyce Wieland, Arthur Lipsett, Jack Chambers, Mike Hoolboom, and R. Bruce Elder. Rimmer emerged among the ranks of those filmmakers that Maria Insell calls the "first generation" of structuralist or materialist filmmakers in Vancouver—among whom she also counts Kirk Tougas, Tom Braidwood, Ellie Epp, Al Razutis, Chris Gallagher, and Peter Lipskis—against the supportive background of the city's art cooperative, Intermedia, headed up by Razutis.

Cinematic form and the cinematic apparatus for structuralist-materialist filmmakers—not the individual consciousness—were the source of perception and meaning, not empty containers for delivering them. Materialist film therefore was film about a critical embrace of the interference of the filmic process itself in the received meanings of the audience. In Rimmer's films this investigation comes through a stylistic usage of found footage and repetition. Both have a central place in what are perhaps his two most well-known works, *Surfacing on the Thames* (1970) and *Variations on a Cellophane Wrapper*

(1970). Through such strategies, combined with a technical versatility in optical and contact printing, re-photography, and rear projection, Rimmer's work blurs the boundaries between the still and the moving image, taking advantage of the historical and visual gaps between static footage and the dynamic narrative that emerges from it through manipulation and looping.

Rimmer himself, in this volume's interview with Alex MacKenzie, acknowledges the influences of filmmaker Stan Brakhage and, surprisingly, the choreography of Yvonne Rainer and Merce Cunningham both of whom he encountered in his short time in New York City, where he shot *Real Italian Pizza* (1971). Viewers of Rimmer's earlier works like *Square Inch Field* (1968) and *Migration* (1969) will note this choreographic style in his kinetic use of camera, replete with rapid zooms and blurred pans combined with often mythic and apocalyptic imagery. The source footage employed by Rimmer throughout his corpus of films is just as often achronological as it is anonymous, barely locatable in time or in space whether in his most painterly work, *Surfacing on the Thames* (1970); his reflections on national mythology and spectacle in *Watching for the Queen* (1973); or in the frivolous *The Dance* (1970). An experimentalist even today, directly applying colour on 35mm film in films like *An Eye for an Eye* (2003), a review of many of Rimmer's earlier films such as *Migration* (1969), *Landscape* (1968), *Canadian Pacific I* (1974) and *Canadian Pacific II* (1975) set his work in sharp relief against the common structuralist penchant for indoor scenarios and confined settings, and constantly return us to the cultural contexts and broad visual "scapes" of Vancouver and British Columbia (both urban and rural) repeatedly invoked throughout his work.

Rimmer's long-spanning creative life, which has mixed film and video work, experimental shorts and feature documentary, and visual and musical subject matter (*Al Neil: A Portrait* [1979]), is—in so many ways—a landmark opportunity to reassess and reengage with Western Canada's contributions to cinema's history: not, of course, as the commercialized "Hollywood North" annex of an increasingly "Global Hollywood" but as one of the most vital, dynamic and productive artistic hubs of twentieth century avant-garde cinema and contemporary independent media.

—Brian Ganter,
Education Department,
Pacific Cinémathèque
Vancouver, 2009

WORKS CITED

Insell, Maria. "Independent Film After Structuralism: Hybrid Experimental Narrative and Documentary." *Vancouver Anthology: The Institutional Politics of Art*. Ed. Stan Douglas. Vancouver: Talonbooks, 1991.

Miller, Toby, et al., ed. *Global Hollywood 2*. London: BFI Publishing, 2005.

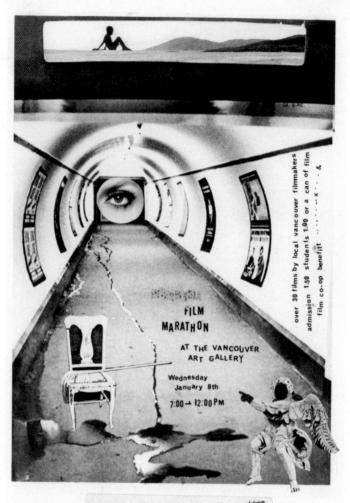

over 30 films by local vancouver filmmakers
admission 1.50 students 1.00 or a can of film
film co-op benefit ....x....&

FILM
MARATHON

AT THE VANCOUVER
ART GALLERY

Wednesday
January 8th

7:00 → 12:00 PM

Photo copy of the poster, designed
and printed by Al Razutis, adver-
tising the Intermedia Film Marathon,
January 8, 1969. *Razutis 60*

David!

BY MIKE HOOLBOOM

TUNE IN, TURN ON

When I asked my friend Richard if he felt he was part of the 'avant-garde' he took a step back and exclaimed, "Avant-garde! That's like the original six teams in hockey. It ended when I was a kid." Oh yes, the fabled avant-garde, home at last in the twentieth century, and raised to feverish heights in the sixties with its dreams of feminism and black power and free love and hand-cranked Bolex cameras to make a picture of it all. We would make our own media, tune in, turn on and drop out. And once we were out, far out, our third eyes would show us the visions of the avant-garde and they would look like home movies. Like home.

Where is our revolution now?

There is a small gaggle of folks still carrying the dream. After all this time bent behind cameras, they can shoot a movie without using one at all; they just swivel their heads and watch it come down twenty four times a second. Thirty if they've switched over to video.

They've managed to live outside as a collective looking in for how many years now? Their look is already a refusal. It is not television for instance, it is not us, all at the same time, saying yes. It's me and it's you, her and him. This is what they believe, these grey hairs, these stooped, balding remnants of revolutions past: that everyone needs to

FACING PAGE: POSTER FOR INTERMEDIA FILM MARATHON, 1969.

look for themselves. There is no uniform law, no ten commandments or reliable science. If it's repeatable, forget about it, throw it away and start over until you can't turn the same number over and over.

Who are they? The ones who don't fit in mostly, geeks and misfits and it's hard to keep that up past forty. When you're twenty it's charming, at thirty it's eccentric, at forty a societal danger, by fifty it's no use, they'll never learn. When you're twenty and soaked in enough beer to preserve flesh into the next century and you get up for a naked jog around the bar it's charming, it's funny, ha-ha, pour the lad another and send him home. Try the same number when you're sixty and the cops are bundling you into the back of the car, no questions asked. Any child past the age of forty should have the decency to stay out of sight, even in the hardly-there scrums of fringe media. Just ask Jack Smith.

Artists rarely have a chance to get old in this country. They give up, or head south, or turn their work into a parlour trick for the agencies if they're really lucky. Mostly other things get in the way. Like family. Trying to make the rent. Security, dying parents, AIDS, the abortion, it means exactly the same thing in the end: no time to make art. That's a luxury, an extra. If youth is wasted on the young, then art is not far behind.

LONG DISTANCE

It's late Friday afternoon in Gastown and I'm standing with my friend Alex outside a micro cinema he's called The Blinding Light!! He explains to me that the window we're settled against was busted up just a couple of weeks back so that someone could grab a handful of CDs that were sitting on the counter. He tells me this with a voice that leans hard into a couple of words, letting me know that if these strangers were music lovers he'd understand, Alex can understand almost anything done in the name of love. But knock down a big beautiful window like that so you can pocket a few CDs and make ten bucks for the next hit? This is capitalism at its most disappointing.

Who walks round the corner right then but David Rimmer. "Mike!" "David!" When I talk to him he looks at me with eyes that never should have been allowed to get quite that blue, and he looks from a long way away. He's standing up in front of me and we're so close I can feel the breath leaving him in even measures, as if someone were inside counting. "Mike!" "David!" I don't know David so well but he likes to talk like that sometimes, in brief exclamation points. And then he goes far away again. He's long distance, he's way out there. Standing here in front of me. Where has he gone? He is trying to pull me into focus from that faraway place and it's hard. I can tell the dream he's leaving has to be pretty sweet because of the effort it requires to get him back here, right here, and then he takes all the time that is in his face and covers me with it and we stand in this luxury of time like two kings. Where did all this time come from? At last there is time to speak and to say the right thing and the wrong one and take one detour, and then another because that's where all the juice is. David knows that so well—the juice is in the detours not the straight lines. If you want it bad enough you stay off the roads. There's nothing on the roads but other drivers. That's US looking again, that's the way WE think, and David's already left US and WE behind. That's what makes him an artist, his knack for wandering, taking the unlikely detour. He explores chance systematically.

MAKING MOVIES

When David started making movies he would take small bits of other people's movies, leftovers, really no more than a metre or two of film and he would look at them for a long time. When he was young he already had the knack of looking at small things for a long time.

WATCHING FOR THE QUEEN, 1973

He wouldn't make a big production out of gathering, he wasn't a hoarder or collector, he didn't need to have everything, there was no set he was trying to complete. He took what was coming to him, and if it wasn't all that much, no worries, that was fine too.

He was a recycler, working with remnants until the audience could feel it right along with him, holding that bit of plastic in his hands. He might dissolve one frame into the next frame into the next, so you'd slowly watch a barge cross the River Thames, along with a storm of golden dust and scratches (*Surfacing on the Thames*, 1970). Or he might make a loop and lay some math on it, showing us a frame for how many seconds, and then the next frame for a bit less and so on, as if each frame were an event, an occasion. Happy Birthday frame (*Watching for the Queen*, 1973)! Or he might make a loop out of a woman throwing some cellophane on a table and then unravel every possible variation, in every colour and combination of colours (*Variations on a Cellophane Wrapper*, 1970). The way he could measure time and rhyme it out second after second like a musician working off a riff, like old Bach sitting down at the clavier running out his variations. David could make the fragments sing.

HANDS

David has these large hands and who knows if it's true but this is the fantasy: he has dad's hands. If anything goes wrong, if the roof leaks or the TV is broken or the washing machine won't start, no problem: these hands are going to fix everything. Thanks dad. These hands are also a way of knowing through touch, understanding directly, up close and personal. We don't need to talk about it, never mind about the manual, the way it's supposed to be done (that's more of the WE version), these hands will find a way. For the last four decades these hands have attached themselves to an art of machines. The interlocking gears, the belts and drives, the old world of industrial hopes and class struggle and the birth of the unconscious, all that is worked on up inside these machines of cinema, and David's hands pass through all that, feeling right at home.

HOME MOVIES

Like every dad he likes to make home movies. How much of the Canadian fringe is home movies? There are the diary boys of the escarpment school, the video narcissists, the coming out movies (coming out gay or nerd or Japanese), the trips back "home" to some far flung part of the (not quite post-colonial) world. But pictures of home have invaded even the work of hard-core conceptual artists like Mike Snow: what else is *Wavelength* (1967) but a long look at home? This is a home that would come to belong to David too. As a young artist he did the right thing and rushed down to New York. Mike was living in a big beautiful loft in the village, and when it was time to leave he gave it to David. A year later it was on the cover of *Artforum*.

Home spun. Home truths. Home made. The Canadian fringe is homemade.

NEW YORK

While David was in New York he set his camera up by one of his windows, looking at the pizza joint across the street. "Real Italian Pizza," the sign read. All kinds of things are happening across New York City but David makes his stand right there, at home. He sets his camera up and that's where he stayed, week after week, month after month, always shooting through the same frame. And in the middle of that frame: Real Italian Pizza (*Real Italian Pizza*, 1971). What a beautiful film it is, ten minutes of summer and fall, with the folks gathered or passing by, the police and fire trucks, the hipsters and not so hip, they're all there. When he gets back to Vancouver he takes an apartment in old Gastown and sets his camera up again. This time he's looking out over railyard and harbour, with the ocean freighters coming to dock and the mountains behind all that. Big weather (*Canadian Pacific*, 1974; *Canadian Pacific II*, 1975). David's running all over the city getting into scenes and falling in love and talking whenever he has to but his camera stays at home, looking out over the docks, shooting when the light is right, or when the fog rolls in, or whenever something catches his eye. He exposes a few frames and then he leaves it alone and goes about his living. This living is also a way of seeing.

AL NEIL

It must have been on one of those all night, steady-on-up-to-the-bar occasions when he met Al Neil. A veteran prankster, Al belonged to another generation, more beat than hippie, playing an off-kilter bebop piano in a style no one had a name for. Maybe they recognized in each other the same kind of being alone and out of this recognition and friendship came David's movie, *Al Neil: A Portrait* (1979). This one really shook me when I saw it, because I'd seen David do his magic act with remaindered footage, spinning it out into something beautiful and precise. But this was documentary territory, this was the Real, the Other, and all those geek chops, all those knowing dad hands, weren't supposed to be able to prep you for encounters like this. Usually the fringe folks would obliterate their subjects with technique, just bury them in flash and flicker, but not David.

In this portrait of his friend he leaves out most of the stuff you're supposed to put in a doc, all the experts and important people telling you how ahead of it all Al's always been. Or people telling you what you're listening to and what you're looking at, parsing the moment. Instead, David films Al close-up playing the lonely piano for a long time. David watches his comrade play, and gives us time to hear him. It keeps on coming at you and it's not the backdrop for the credits— it's the thing itself. He shoots nearly the whole movie inside Al's strange ramble of a house. We see the totems he's carved and for a few moments Al talks his talk in that raspy unforgettable voice, coming through the years and the good bottle David's brought along to make it smooth. Al's laugh: like a coffin heading the wrong way. And then right at the end of the movie we see him at a packed gathering in a gallery called Pumps, and it's a shock. All of a sudden Al's up onstage at the head of a buzz and he's got a little serial music in his mouth, he's going to start off with some Steve Reich ideas he

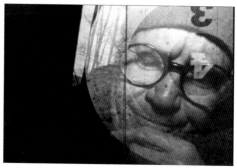

AL NEIL: A PORTRAIT, 1979

exclaims, and sure enough he does. But inside a few bars he's back to playing that strange, tortured bebop we've been hearing for the last half hour, and even though it's running out over the crowd we're inside the music, we're close to these familiar notes, we've found a new home here.

As an artist who makes pictures David has one great advantage which is that he hardly knows how to talk. Never trusted words. All that wind out of the mouth. He can't fill in the place his pictures should live by talking himself out of it or talking until the feeling stops entirely. He wouldn't know where to begin. He keeps his mouth shut and his camera open.

FILM AND VIDEO

David was never part of fringe media's cold war: film versus video. He did a few turns with video back in New York for instance, shooting some of the right now with the weight lifting machines that passed for video recorders in those days. So maybe it was no big surprise that he hit the 1980s with a video recorder in one hand and a Bolex in the other. But slowly those tight little film circles he was running as a young man got worked up alongside other kinds of loops, and while these moments never collected into anything like storyland, some idea of purity had been left behind so he could chase down other dreams. David was still looking hard at small bits of thrown away media, but instead of running them through their paces and showing what pictures looked like when they were left to play, he wanted to rub them up together until he had something like montage. And in order to pull these pictures out of the trash pile once and for all he had to get them to look different, to look the way he was seeing them all along, and in order to do that he needed video.

What he was trying to do with his film/video hybrids like *As Seen on TV* (1986) was keep himself up on the wire. The truth is, he'd found his way early and got right down and painted his masterpieces in the ten shorts he pulled out of his hat between 1970-74. Then he trumped his own trick four years later with *Al Neil: A Portrait*. Most artists would have the dignity to quit, to pack up and change careers, but David went on, though it took him a few years to find a new groove. He was still committed to the short form; paintings weren't any better if they took up the whole ceiling. So he lays a snippet of epileptic seizure between day-glo-coloured TV bits until the seizure becomes a comment on televisual spasm which he names *As Seen on TV*. He runs a loop of sound and picture out of joint until the sound comes all the way back and accompanies the picture again in *Bricolage* (1984). Sometimes it can take

AS SEEN ON TV, 1986

that long, require that many attempts, until you see a picture at all. In *Narrows Inlet* (1980) he takes his camera out on a boat and click clicks a frame at a time even though he can't glimpse a thing. He's caught in the fog and there's nothing there at all until a sliver of colour appears, and then slowly, oh so very slowly, the fog lifts and the tree line lives again, staring back at the camera with all of its colour and height resolved. Another small miracle of looking.

By the end of the 1980s he's in China, replaying the last twenty years of his life in the movies, only with Chinese crowds pulling themselves into his lens. *Black Cat White Cat It's a Good Cat If It Catches the Mouse* (1989) asks: How do I look? He takes it all in with steady precision, up early each morning to catch the only light worth gazing into, except for the last moments of the day, so he climbs back to catch some of that too, finding his way between sleepers and trains and tai chi circuits. He meets his subject halfway, not you over there like a zoo specimen, but both of us inside the cage, checking each other out, making contact. David has a knack for finding the necessary distance.

Without that distance, it's impossible to begin looking. Every day tourists are busy turning cameras on but it's no use, they manage to record everything without seeing a thing. Most artists, never mind tourists, are still trying to find the distance. David is busy showing us how.

His second great "period" comes to an end with *Local Knowledge* (1992). It is a reckoning and last stand. Not a movie that could ever be made by a young man, its time-compressed skies and hunters and fishers and motorboat reveries narrate a home movie reading of the west coast. Beautiful pictures, one after another, but more than that. He wants to let go because letting go feels like freedom, only it's not. David's been around long enough to know that too. Freedom arrives in the net, the frame. Only when the taboo and prohibition have been drawn is the artist free to play. That's the sad, long lesson of *Local Knowledge*. Hard because you can't smile with the same sort of innocence after that.

David has made many movies since *Local Knowledge*, though none with its urgency or scale. It's hard to stay up on the wire as long as he has. No one's managed it longer in this country. He's still looking for a way back, trying to feel his way through paint splatters on frozen emulsion, or another good look at the landscape around him, or another fascinated discard of footage. He's been there and back and knows the only place where he's worth a damn is moving moments together that don't belong, looking into faces for a long time until he can see clear through them to the other side. He's the youngest older person I know. Finally retired from teaching, he can give that old dog a rest, and with all that new time settling in, who knows what's next?

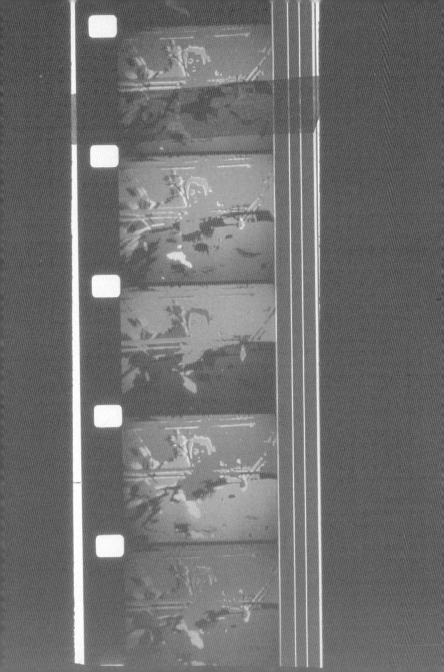

Variations on a Celluloid Wrapper

ALEX MACKENZIE INTERVIEWS DAVID RIMMER

MacKenzie: Let's just start by asking you, David, how you came to the kind of work that you do. Did you come to it honestly?

Rimmer: Out of necessity, I guess. Gee, where to start? I guess I'll start by talking about how I got involved in film, and why. I was at UBC [University of British Columbia]. I graduated from UBC in economics.

MacKenzie: Oh. Economics.

Rimmer: And math. And decided before I got down to work I wanted to travel. So I took two years and I hitchhiked around the world. All through Asia, India, and Afghanistan, the Middle East, most of Europe, Africa—right down to Capetown. And that took two years, and I got back to Vancouver thinking, "Well, I really don't want to be a businessman," which is what I was trained for, I guess, in economics. It didn't seem very interesting, and I'd seen the rest of the world and I thought, "Well, there's much more interesting things to do, but what am I going to do?" […] So I went back to UBC and did a degree in English. Which meant a couple of years of straight English courses. And ended up at Simon Fraser [University], started doing an MA in English, taking a course on Ezra Pound from Robin Blaser.

FACING PAGE: VARIATIONS ON A CELLOPHANE WRAPPER, 1970.

But I wasn't very comfortable doing that, because I wasn't myself a writer. And I really couldn't see myself spending my life studying other writers. But I didn't know what else there was. That's why I went into English, because it seemed somewhat interesting. And I remember, sitting around in a seminar, a graduate seminar one day, and looking around at the people, and thinking, y'know—"What's everybody gonna do with all this?" […] And I had got somewhat interested in film when I was at UBC. I used to go to the Cinema 16 Film Society which ran screenings every week. So I'd seen Dada films, Surrealist films, the usual stuff. And decided, "Hey, let's make a film." And I had a camera. I bought a camera in Gibraltar while I was traveling. And so I got together with some friends, and we tried to make a Surrealist film out of complete naivety. And it didn't really work, but it was kind of interesting. It piqued my interest. So I started playing around more with film. 8mm.

MacKenzie: Now was this your first foray into any kind of artistic practice?

Rimmer: Yeah. I mean, that was part of a thing on wondering what to do, because I'd never been that interested in art, or had made it even. So it wasn't even an option. I went towards English, because it was more academic. And then one day, Stan Brakhage came to UBC and showed *Dogstar Man*. I remember sitting in a classroom in the Buchanan building, and Brakhage came in the back door and he had this long hair, and beard, and a bandolier around him, around his shoulders. Instead of bullets in the bandolier, he had hundred-foot film cans.

MacKenzie: Always the showman.

Rimmer: Yeah, always the showman. So he showed this film *Dogstar Man* and I thought, "What the fuck is this all about? I've never seen anything like this." It was completely different than what I'd been used to with Surrealist Dada films. And I said, "I don't know what he's doing, but it's interesting." And then, a friend of mine—Gerry Gilbert, who's a poet—said, "Hey, look at this book, you might be interested," and he gave me Brakhage's *Metaphors on Vision*, which he'd written about the same time as he was making *Dogstar Man*. And I opened this book up, and the first page it said something like, "Imagine an eye un-ruled by compositional logic." […] "How many shades of green are there to a child who has no conception of green?" I went, "Gee, this is interesting." So I read this whole book. And what it showed me was that anything was possible in film. Anything. I remember him saying, he said, "Spit on the lens and then shoot and see what happens . . . throw the

MIGRATION, 1969

camera in the air . . . do everything wrong and see what happens." So, I thought, "Well, I'll try this." […] So I made a couple of early films—*Square Inch Field* and *Migration*—that were quite influenced by Brakhage. Particularly *Migration*, the way I was cutting and editing, very sort of fast, rhythmic editing . . . lots of blurs and what not […] It seemed to be something I could do, that I had some talent for, that I hadn't realized before. That I somehow understood the visual language better than the written, spoken language . . . the "word" language. So I kept doing it.

» » »

Rimmer: Before I went to New York, I was involved with a group in Vancouver called Intermedia, and Intermedia was a Canada Council-funded sort of arts lab, an arts workshop where the idea was to bring together artists from different disciplines, and see how they work together. So there was poets, there was painters, there was performance artists, there was filmmakers, there was photographers, musicians. […] And we would do a number of, we did a number of really large shows at the old Vancouver Art Gallery where we would install work, we would do performance, we would do music, we would do projections, the whole works. And again, that was like part of my education, too. See, I never went to art school.

MacKenzie: Was it a time where—it seems to me now trying to do something like that at the Vancouver Art Gallery would be a real trick.

Rimmer: It was a really open time at the Vancouver Art Gallery. Tony Emery was the Director at that time and Doris Shadbolt was the Head Curator—and they would say, "C'mon in!" We could go . . . I remember going once with Don Druick and Taki Bluesinger. We had an idea for a show. We went to Doris. We just walked right in to Doris' office, which you can't do now. "Doris, what do you think of this?" She says, "Great, when do you want to do it?" So we did it. So they were incredibly open and encouraging.

» » »

About that time, Al Razutis came up from LA: he was dodging the draft. He was making experimental films. He knew a little more about it than I did because he lived in California where things were going on. And he began to bring in programs of experimental films to Intermedia. So I got to see people like Pat O'Neil and the Whitney brothers and—who are the other people in that era? Scott Bartlett, Bruce Connor.

MacKenzie: [Paul] Sharits, maybe?

Rimmer: Not Sharits yet, no, 'cause he was in the East Coast. And I thought, "Gee, these guys are interesting." Razutis would bring more stuff up, and we'd look at more stuff. So I remember deciding one day, sitting in my English graduate seminar, that I was going to leave. I was going to quit school, and I was going to try and make films. See what would happen.

MacKenzie: And Intermedia's being operated by a collective kind of set-up? Everyone's getting in on the action?

Rimmer: Yeah.

MacKenzie: So were there artists working there that were having an impact on you in the same way that the artists in New York later would? Or did that come later?

Rimmer: Well, they were artists but not filmmakers. They were Intermedia. There was myself, Razutis, Gary Lee-Nova, [producer, director and writer] Tom Shandel, working in film . . . and probably some others I've forgotten. But most of them were other kinds of artists. A lot of performance was going on.

MacKenzie: And were these people having an influence on the directions you were taking at the time?

Rimmer: Oh yeah. 'Cause I was then, y'know, my work was coming from an art background rather than a film background. Rather than trying to learn how to make dramatic film or documentary, or going to film school—there was no film school then, fortunately. If I'd have had to go to film school, I would have turned out completely differently, I'm sure.

MacKenzie: Or you would've left film school.

Rimmer: Or I would've left film school. But there wasn't a film school. We were also working with video, then, and I think this is important, that this was like the late sixties, early seventies— and Intermedia had acquired from Sony the loan of a half-inch black-and-white port-a-pack. Very heavy thing. Black and white. Twenty minute tapes. Almost impossible to edit. I mean, you could, initially; you edited by taping, by splicing.

MacKenzie: Cutting them—

Rimmer: Cutting it and actually sticking some sticky tape down.

So we played with these machines. I found a way of doing double exposures on these machines. By covering the erase head with a piece of plastic, and shooting something, and covering it, and shooting it again, I would get a double exposure. [...] It was messy. And then when I went to New York, I was working in video, too.

» » »

Rimmer: [A]bout that time, my wife at the time, Karen Jamieson, who's a dancer—choreographer—had decided to go to New York and study. She said, "You want to come? Let's go to New York." I said, "Great, let's go to New York." [...] We didn't have much money. I was driving a taxi to survive, then. So I applied for a Canada Council grant, and it was called at that time an "arts bursary." And it was thirty-seven-hundred dollars a year, no matter what discipline you're in. [...] So I applied. I remember getting the application form and looking down the form and it said, "Discipline: painting, sculpture, music, writing," and I said, "Well, it doesn't say film on here anywhere." So I wrote, "film." I drew a little box and checked it off. And sent this thing in. And to my utter amazement, I got the grant. And that was enough to take me to New York, where quite quickly I got to know people there who were involved in the art of film—like Sharits and those kind of people. Tony Conrad and Stan Lawder and people, and began to get my own work shown. [...] I showed at places like Millennium and MoMA. Peter Feinstein was just opening the Film Forum up on the Upper West Side. There was a lot of activity going on. I stayed there for three years, and over those three years I really got to see most of the work that was going on in the States, and meet most of the filmmakers. Because everybody came through New York to do shows. So that was my education in film.

» » »

Rimmer: That was an interesting influence too—being in New York and learning something about the dance scene, because [Karen] was studying with people like Merce Cunningham. And there was a lot of activity in New York, y'know, at that time. Cunningham and Cage and all sorts of performance work going on, and . . . .

MacKenzie: There was generally more of a vibrant, sort of crossover of zones, it seems.

Rimmer: Yeah. Yvonne Rainer, y'know, I danced with Yvonne Rainer—in performance. My brief dance career. Then came back and just started, just kept making films, really.

» » »

Rimmer: While I was living in New York, actually, I went to Europe a couple of times because the Filmmaker's Co-Op in London was running what they called an "underground film festival" every couple of years. I was invited to that, where I had a chance then to meet most of the European experimental filmmakers. The Germans, the English, the French, Eastern European even, at that time. So I came back from New York to Vancouver with some kind of knowledge of what was going on, and a lot more confidence in what I was doing. Knowing that I could survive too, and that there was a community of people who were trying to push the boundaries of film and video.

MacKenzie: And you felt like you could play a part in that?

Rimmer: Yeah. It seemed much more comfortable to me, or interesting to me, than going into the film industry.

MacKenzie: Which was—was that even ever an option for you?

Rimmer: Well, I actually . . . yeah, it was in a sense. I worked for about six months at CBC [Canadian Broadcasting Corporation], CBC Television, through a guy called Stan Fox who was very supportive in the early days of film. And I started out as a negative cutter, at CBC. Then I graduated to editor. One day, they said, "You're an editor now." I remember a producer came in and he threw this stuff on my desk and he said, "Sync these up, and I'll be back at lunchtime." Alright. Okay. I said, "Sync these up? What the fuck does that mean?" So I went to an editor next door, who was Ray Hall. Another supportive CBC guy. I said, "What's this 'sync up' stuff? How do I do it?" So he showed me how to do it. Very quickly. Y'know, it meant synching up mag and 16mm reversal film with a synchronizer, a little viewer and a squawk box. So I cut a number of sort of news documentaries at CBC. And it was interesting, but that was about the time I decided to go to New York—so I sort of quit that job.

MacKenzie: Was that your last contact with people like Stan, who are involved at CBC? In terms of support? Or did you return to that?

Rimmer: Umm . . . .

MacKenzie: Like, when you say they're supportive, do you mean—

Rimmer: Well, Stan and another guy called Gene Lawrence, started a couple of TV programs, late night TV programs: one called *Enterprise* and one called . . . something else. I can't remember what it is. So, they had given out film to a group of us. Tom Shandel was one of these people. Out of date film, you know—they'd pay for the processing, they'd give us some access to the editing room. And we made these films. That's where I made *Square Inch Field* and *Migration* for CBC. And showed them on CBC.

MacKenzie: So, the equivalent of what? A cable access kind of quality these days, in terms of the accessibility of it. I mean, there's no way you'd get in to CBC like that.

Rimmer: No, there's no way you can now. It was more enlightened then. Got a job at UBC in the Fine Arts department for a few years, and then went over to Simon Fraser for a few years, and Emily Carr [Institute of Art & Design] for a few more years. And just kept working, really.

MacKenzie: And the dynamism that you're finding with Intermedia, before you left, and then upon your return, what was the shape of that? Did it continue on?

Rimmer: No. It sort of petered out. We all got tired of it.

MacKenzie: Too much work, or?

Rimmer: I don't know. It was really intensive for about four years, maybe. Four or five years. And everybody got sort of burnt out, and people wanted to go off and do their own things. So, I remember we decided as a group, "Let's disband it."

Then, we phoned the Canada Council and said, "Don't send any more money."

MacKenzie: "We're done."

Rimmer: "We're done!"

» » »

MacKenzie: It sounds like you had a supportive community at that time, and the newness of it maybe helped it fly. Y'know? Like, "Hey, here's something that no one even thought about before," and so there was room for that. But, did you feel at the time that you were up against challenges that you felt maybe other practices weren't?

Rimmer: To a certain extent. I mean, even photography was not accepted as a real art form and certainly not experimental film. The galleries dealt with painting and sculpture. But we created our own galleries created our own spaces. Y'know, we would take over a storefront. I remember Razutis and I and [filmmaker] Keith Rodan made a little theatre down on Main Street, and we advertised it. We got closed down by the police, the Fire Marshal, and we couldn't, we couldn't do . . . This was interesting because we'd set this whole thing up, "Razutis, Rimmer, Rodan" posters everywhere, made this theatre, got some seats, just like you did at the Blinding Light!!

MacKenzie: Or earlier at the Edison. Probably more like the Edison, yeah?

Rimmer: Yeah. And the fire marshal came in, just, y'know, on the afternoon of the show and said, "No, you can't do it. You don't have this. You don't have that." […] So we went up to the Vancouver Art Gallery, and we saw probably Doris Shadbolt, and we said, "Doris, we got a problem." She said, "Oh, show it here." So, y'know, within a few hours we had changed venues and we were in the Vancouver Art Gallery. And we showed it there. So they were really supportive, it's that—maybe the other galleries, the commercial galleries, didn't want anything to do with it. But Doris did, and Tony, and Jack Shadbolt was very supportive, too.

MacKenzie: I mean, it raises an interesting question about economics, and the economics of experimental filmmaking, and that commercial galleries aren't likely to have an interest because there's nothing to sell.

Rimmer: There's nothing to sell. Right.

MacKenzie: And, I mean, that's definitely a challenge, I think, of most people working in this "zone," is, you don't have paintings to sell, you have nothing to pass on economically, and so how do you survive in that realm? And obviously, y'know, some teach, some do something else entirely.

» » »

MacKenzie: So did you feel like you had to teach? Were you interested in teaching at that time?

Rimmer: Yeah, I was interested in it. And again, that was more my education. Teaching, I learned, y'know, because I was working with other artists and painters and academics, etcetera. I learned a lot by doing that. So it was good in that way.

MacKenzie: And at that time, you say UBC was, open to possibilities and different arenas of art-making and practice and visitors. Do you remember a time when that started to change? When things like the gallery and the universities became less open to that? Or was it gradual? And was there something about the general Zeitgeist that was changing?

Rimmer: I don't know. It sort of petered out at UBC. I don't quite know why. In terms of the film department, I was the only one at UBC who was talking about experimental film. The other film department in theatre was more concerned with dramatics. So when I left UBC, there was nobody there—

MacKenzie: To fill your shoes.

Rimmer: To fill my shoes. [...] So, I moved over to Simon Fraser and there happened to be a space there. And it was happening more there. The energy had gone . . . .

MacKenzie: Well, things were picking up at that time at SFU, I think.

Rimmer: Yeah.

MacKenzie: Yeah. And was Al there at that time?

Rimmer: And Razutis was there causing all sorts of havoc as usual. Confronting everybody and everything as he does, as he still does.

MacKenzie: And so that was a lively time at SFU?

Rimmer: Yeah, it was a lively time. Yeah. It's funny, I still see a lot of those students. A lot of them have continued to work, not necessarily in experimental—but independent film, independent features, independent documentaries, working for the film board, etcetera.

MacKenzie: They didn't disappear.

Rimmer: No. No, there's a lot of them still here.

» » »

MacKenzie: So you picked up at Emily Carr?

Rimmer: Mmm hmm.

MacKenzie: And I think at that time, Emily Carr was becoming, it seems to me, more of a happening place. Maybe more, I don't know, "street level," or willing to pursue things that the more already long-institutionalized zones weren't. Like UBC and SFU.

Rimmer: Well, it wasn't a university. It was an art school.

MacKenzie: Right.

Rimmer: So people were coming from the art world rather than the film world.

MacKenzie: And it was specifically an art school as opposed to universities that have all sorts of departments.

Rimmer: Yeah. It didn't have a lot of academic courses in those days; it was much more practical.

MacKenzie: And there was room there for your practice and interests?

Rimmer: Yeah, I was hired actually as a video teacher. That was, the video instructor had gone or something, and so there was a hole there. But the situation there at Emily Carr in those days was there was a number of us teaching in the film department—I don't remember what it was called then—and it all overlapped. So although I was the video teacher, I would work with the experimental film people.

» » »

MacKenzie: Let's maybe start talking about your films in particular.

Rimmer: Okay.

MacKenzie: Some of your films are short and explore single moments, stretching them out in various ways, while your longer works use different strategies to render their gestures and build their arcs. Could you tell me about your process and how it varies from one film to the next?

Rimmer: Oh boy.

MacKenzie: It's a big question, feel free to answer it in small pieces. You spoke a bit about the very early work, I guess helped along by access to materials and Stan Fox and the CBC. Beyond that, how did things begin to come together for you in creating a work?

Rimmer: I don't know. I guess the works sort of grew—always seemed to grow—out of things I'm interested in and that I'm, say, reading about, or thinking about. And I begin to sort of pull in images that somehow relate to what I'm thinking about, and I'm using these images to try to understand what I'm thinking about also. So initially, well, near the very beginning I began working the loops. And I guess the most well-known film in that genre is *Variations on* *a Cellophane Wrapper*. And where did that come from? That grew out of me first of all finding this very nice loop. It was a loop of—a strip of film of a woman in a factory who was shaking out big sheets of cellophane. And it was a perfect loop in the sense that it was hard to tell where the cut was, because she . . .

MacKenzie: Right. It joins nicely.

Rimmer: It does, and then it cuts, and she does it again and it cuts, and she does it again. And I really liked this image so I started making copies of it and printing it, and printing it on negative, and printing it on high contrast, and printing it with colour filters, and just seeing where it was going. And I used it a lot in—we would do these Intermedia performance events where we might have four or six projectors going, 16mm projectors going, and a poet reading and a musician playing. So I used these in performance. And then I thought maybe I should just fix this into an actual film before I wear out all these loops. So I did. I kind of strung different bits together. And the idea was to take this image and just disintegrate it over time. Do as many things that I could to it to see where it would lead. And as I began to do that, the image, the meaning of the image would change. Initially it was just the image itself that interested me as a physical thing. And then I began, and people would say, "Oh, that's about this or that's about that." And I'd say, "Okay, that's interesting." People who are poetically inclined would see it as the woman trapped in the factory. She also looked at some point like a dancing Shiva. So people who are oriented that way would see it in those terms. So I thought, "This is interesting because there's a number of different interpretations, and I want to leave it

VARIATIONS ON A CELLOPHANE WRAPPER, 1970

open. So I just did it. I just made the thing. But whenever I'm working with loops I look at the stuff over and over and over again until it starts to kind of speak back to me. Rather than trying to impose an idea or a theory on it before I've made it.

MacKenzie: So you're looking—physically you're creating a loop and looking at it over and over again?

Rimmer: Yeah.

MacKenzie: Or are you going back and forth over the material on a Steenbeck [editing table]?

Rimmer: No, I'd be looking at it on a projector, and we didn't have Steenbecks then. We did, but I didn't have access to them.

MacKenzie: Right. And when you say you found this "perfect loop" how did you find that loop? That piece?

Rimmer: Well, that's a story too, because we used to get a lot of stock footage to play with, and we'd get it from CBC. We knew where they stored the film they were going to throw out. It was in this garage behind the CBC. We'd go in and we'd steal the film. The Film Board also—when their prints had worn out—and it was all 16mm in those day—they'd throw them out. Somehow we were there to get them or they would even donate them to Intermedia and say, "Here's something to play with." So we'd look through this stuff and pull stuff out and make loops and whatnot. But with the *Cellophane Wrapper* one it came out of a Film Board film. And, just a brief story: I remember once the National Film Board at the end of their budget year was giving out some money to independent filmmakers, not much, two hundred, three hundred, four hundred dollars. So I went into this—made an appointment to meet with Peter Jones who was the head of the Film Board at that time, and I didn't know Peter then. I knew who he was. And I remember going into the screening room with him and I was feeling quite intimidated. Here was Peter Jones, head of the Film Board. He had a suit on, the works. And he says, "Okay, show me what you've got here." So I showed him *Variations on a Cellophane Wrapper*, kind of a rough cut of it with no sound or nothing. Said I wanted to get some money to make a release print. As soon as it came on he started laughing and chuckling and giggling. I thought, "Oh fuck! He doesn't like it. He thinks it's stupid. I shouldn't have come in here." And after, he said, he turned to me and said, "Where'd you get that image?" And I said, "Well, I don't know. Somewhere. Some stock footage I found." He said, "I shot that."

MacKenzie: Wow. That's hilarious.

Rimmer: Because he had been a cameraman before he was the head of the Board. And he thought it was the funniest thing that I had found this and made this out of it, and he gave me three hundred dollars to make the release print.

MacKenzie: Great.

Rimmer: So that was sort of indirect encouragement from the Film Board. But the Film Board in those days was actually a lot easier to get involved in.

MacKenzie: Yeah.

Rimmer: You know, they would let you into their Steenbecks at night to work. They were supportive. It's getting much harder for them now because their money's getting cut back all the time. And I think they would still like to help people a lot but they just don't have the—

MacKenzie: The funds.

Rimmer: The funding to do it properly, and film is getting so expensive now. I mean, we would make films for nothing. It's just like now you can make video for nothing, and that's one reason I'm working in video a lot now.

» » »

MacKenzie: *Square Inch Field* and *Migration*: you spoke a bit about them earlier and working with Stan Fox and getting access that way. Your style of editing obviously takes a central role, in camera and post, that overwhelms and transports the viewer. Can you talk a bit about the process in making these works with regards to that editing? I think *Square Inch Field*—was that largely in-camera?

Rimmer: Some of it was. I can't remember now. But both of those films sort of grew out of some images that I had. Particularly *Migration*, which owes a lot to Brakhage's ideas about editing. I found a dead deer on the beach one day, I was living up in Indian Arm—and I shot this deer and that became sort of the centre of this film, and then I worked on either side of that editing material, right? So that came first and that kind of inspired . . .

MacKenzie: That was the central motif. Right. Okay.

Rimmer: And there were sort of clichés, things like earth, water, fire and air, that kind of stuff. Which I'm still interested in in other ways.

MacKenzie: They're clichés for a reason.

Rimmer: Yeah. But I often don't know where the films are going. I think if I did, you know, they'd be weak films.

MacKenzie: But I guess it does help to have that anchor, like the deer.

Rimmer: Yeah. That was the anchor. And in *Square Inch Field* it was the earth, water, fire, and air—it was the kind of structure that I played around with.

MacKenzie: Have you ever begun with a structure, an anchor, and abandoned it? Thinking, "Oh, it got me this far but it's not helping me."

Rimmer: Probably, probably. I don't know. I mean, sometimes I will conceive of a structure before I've made the film—like in *Watching for the Queen*, which is a crowd of people, a few hundred people, all looking at the camera, and they're already looking at the Queen who's going by in a car. And with that what I decided to do was be really structural, so I printed the first frame for one minute, the second frame for half a minute, the third frame for a quarter of a minute until I got down to twenty-four frames a second. So, that was very mathematically worked out.

MacKenzie: Now, it was mathematically worked out, but would you say it was a structural film or was there an emotional impact and—imagining that you had, from the get-go, that you thought, "This is going to look like this and that's going to be interesting in an emotional way"? Did the emotional potential of it shape it or were you just thinking, "This is an experiment, a technical experiment, let's see what happens"?

Rimmer: Well, it was more than a technical experiment because the image of all these people—and they were moving their heads in various ways—was interesting to me, and the idea, like, "What are they looking at?"

MacKenzie: So, yeah, obviously you've chosen that material quite specifically.

Rimmer: And there was a kind of rhythm in how they moved, and when I ran it over and over again, certain people would pop up at certain times.

MacKenzie: But you had to imagine.

Rimmer: Well, I could see it. I mean, I could look at it on a Steenbeck, or on a viewer, really, and get an idea of what it might look like. […] It's not very complicated mathematics. When I made it, it was a matter of punching it out, really, on the optical printer.

» » »

MacKenzie: *Landscape*, remember that film?

Rimmer: Mm hmm.

MacKenzie: This was, apparently, originally intended for rear projection in a gallery setting?

Rimmer: Not originally, but subsequently it was projected.

MacKenzie: So that was its final shape?

Rimmer: Yeah. It was a time lapse over fifteen hours at Storm Bay [near Sechelt, BC] looking out of the bay at some mountains that were various shades of blue and with clouds and everything like that. So I just made it, I thought this would be a neat thing to do, so I did it, you don't think about these things that much. So I did. I sat there for fifteen hours and did it manually because I didn't have a machine.

MacKenzie: Wow. With a watch or just intuitively?

Rimmer: Just, one thousand and one, one thousand and two . . .
[*laughter*]

MacKenzie: For fifteen hours? Did you have a sandwich break?

Rimmer: Yeah, I had people to come and relieve me from time to time while I relieved myself. But, yeah, it was nice to sit, it was very interesting to sit there for fifteen hours. […] I did another time lapse once from Vancouver to Montreal. I set up a camera in my car, and I rigged up this homemade motor to take a frame every ten seconds or something, and we got out to about Hope, I guess, and smoke started coming out of the camera mechanism and the motor burned out. So I had a long cable release and I drove to Montreal with one hand, clicking with the other hand.

MacKenzie: Wow.

Rimmer: On the single frame.

MacKenzie: Every . . . ?

Rimmer: Every ten seconds or so, twenty seconds, I can't remember. And then I got the film back and I thought, "Oh fuck! This is boring as shit! As hell!" and I've never used it. In fact I threw it away when I was cleaning up one day. It just didn't work.

» » »

MacKenzie: *Blue Movie* was originally intended, as I understand it, for your dome where the viewer lies down and looks up to view it. Can you tell me about this dome? I don't know much about the role it played . . .

Rimmer: One of the Intermedia projects we did at the old Vancouver Art Gallery—we did a thing called "The Dome Show" and in every room in the gallery we built a geodesic dome. Some were made out of steel pipes. Some were made out of wood. Some were made out of—mine was made out of cedar strips covered with cloth. And various things went on in these domes: performances or poetry readings, or . . .

MacKenzie: So you could go walk right into them? You were completely encased by them?

Rimmer: Yeah, you could go right in. You could go right into them.

MacKenzie: It wasn't just a ceiling thing that was hanging, or . . . ?

Rimmer: Oh no, no.

MacKenzie: You were right in—

Rimmer: You would go right into it. So my dome was, I think, fifteen feet in diameter or twelve feet in diameter. It was a small dome. And up in the ceiling I had rigged up a 16mm projector. It was projecting down onto the dome and the image was sort of spilling over.

MacKenzie: Stretching across.

Rimmer: Stretching over. And it was images of water, waves,

clouds. All kind of manipulated through some colour separation techniques.

MacKenzie: And you'd be getting the triangular shadows, I guess, of the cedar.

Rimmer: Yeah. Well, the image—the cloth that I covered the thing with—was quite porous so I would get the image on the outside of the dome. But it'd also come through the holes of the cloth and be projected onto the floor, and the floor was covered in some circles of white foam that I scavenged somewhere from some company. And so you could go in and you could sit and you could look up. Jerry Gilbert said it was like looking in your eyeball, at your eyeball. I remember going in there early one morning to check on my loops because they were always breaking, and it was Senior Citizens Day at the gallery and there were all these old senior citizens lying on the floor of the dome looking up. It was beautiful.

MacKenzie: That, that . . . I mean, there was definitely a period in time where the dome was the future. I mean, Buckminster Fuller and his whole strategies of future architecture and then it seemed to wane, and there was this one guy . . . the guy who wrote *Shelter*. He talks about various ways of building on your own, and he also produced a book about dome building, and he actually retracted it at a certain point in history where he said, "You know what? I was wrong. Building a dome is not a good idea. It's not a good way to live. There's all sorts of problems attached to it, so, you know, I've taken—I'm no longer printing this book, it's no longer available and here's the reasons why. Please see my new book."

Rimmer: Interesting.

MacKenzie: Yeah. But the only thing—the only trace of that that we have now is Imax—or sorry, Omnimax, the big round screening rooms and those tend to be fairly broad stroke documentaries about broad stroke non-issue kind of stuff. Do you ever have fantasies about that?

Rimmer: I'd love to do something for that space. I mean, I've been in it a few times to see the shows they put on. I'm not that interested in the content of what they're doing, really. It's spectacular, you know, especially if it's 3-D. But it would be wonderful to get—I think what they should do is give, you know, ten artists a chance to make things for that space, and bring to that various experimental techniques that we've been using and see what will happen.

» » »

MacKenzie: *Real Italian Pizza* was made while you were living in New York, filmed out of your loft window across the street over a period of eight months. While *Canadian Pacific I* and *II* were similarly built in Vancouver at two different times. Can you talk about the actual process here? How much time was spent at the window. The moments chosen and those not. The moments missed. Was it a casual affair?

Rimmer: Okay, well let's start with *Real Italian Pizza*. I'd just moved to New York. We were living on West 85th, Upper West Side, just at the edge of a Puerto Rican neigbourhood. And I wanted to make a film about New York. I didn't know where to start; it's such a big place. And I was a little reluctant to take my camera out on the street because it's a tough place, you know, and a lot of people would try and steal it from me, I guess. And I didn't know the rhythm of the city enough to . . . So I thought, "Why not just stick it out the window?" And fortunately, across the street, this is four floors up, there was a pizza parlour and there was a lot of activity going on in front of it: kids would hang out there, drug deals would go on, or . . .

MacKenzie: Occasionally people would buy pizza.

Rimmer: People would buy pizza. So I thought, "Well, okay, every morning at ten o'clock I will take x number of frames." Then I thought, "No, that's going to be boring as hell because there'd probably be nothing happening."

MacKenzie: Who's buying pizza at ten a.m.?

Rimmer: Yeah. So I thought a much more interesting thing was to leave the camera there and then whenever I go by the window check it out and see if there's something going on and if there was, I'd shoot, and if not I wouldn't. So I didn't need to structure my shooting that much. So I did over those eight months—just kept shooting stuff.

MacKenzie: And you reserved that camera for that purpose?

Rimmer: I could take it off sometimes and put it back. It was easy enough to frame up again, you know. The framing wasn't always perfect. And I was sort of cutting it as I was making it, too. Stringing stuff together, and then—

MacKenzie: You mean literally? Like, processing the film and . . .

Rimmer: I'd process it and then I'd edit that bit in, you know.

MacKenzie: Was this again working off of—with a projector or did you have a Steenbeck, or?

Rimmer: No, I had rewinds—and a viewer. Yeah. And I guess it ended when I left New York in the spring to come back here because . . .

MacKenzie: That was that.

Rimmer: That was it.

MacKenzie: No more time.

» » »

MacKenzie: So, *Canadian Pacific I* and *II*—what did that look like? Was it a similar sort of process as *Real Italian Pizza*?

Rimmer: Yeah. Shooting out the window, there was train tracks . . . trains, the ocean, boats, and the mountains. And, again, just whenever I was around I'd keep my eyes open to see what was happening. If an interesting train going by, or a boat going by, or a cloud formation, or snowing, you know, and I'd shoot . . . I think I'd shoot about ten seconds each time and then I'd just dissolve them all together.

MacKenzie: There's dissolving going on there.

Rimmer: Yeah.

MacKenzie: Was that a new idea for you, or?

Rimmer: I'd used dissolves, but not that much. There must be, I don't know, a couple of hundred dissolves in it. Just dissolving from one to the other. It was a nightmare for the lab to do because they had to set all those things up with timing cues and whatnot. So I did that and then the next year I lost that loft and I moved next door two floors up, and I thought, "Well, I'll make the same movie again," because I was looking at the same . . . but one is, like, looking like that [indicates viewing at an angle] the other one is looking down. So they're the same length. And then I would—I showed those as films but they also have existed in galleries where there's sometimes just one kind of false screen in a wall or sometimes there's two, running on sort of loops.

MacKenzie: Picture frame style?

Rimmer: Yeah. Even when I did it in, I think it was Winnipeg Art Gallery, I had actual picture frames put up in the gallery . . . around them. So they became like, you know, moving paintings.

MacKenzie: Yeah, they're interesting in terms of this, obviously the Vancouver landscape, and having read reviews of them by people who don't know Vancouver, they're kind of blown away by this landscape—and it seems so, well, spectacular and inaccessible, but to you it's right outside your window and it's something very familiar to us living here . . . but it does certainly make you look again, you know, and ponder it, consider it.

» » »

MacKenzie: So just to finish up about both *Real Italian Pizza* and *Canadian Pacific I* and *II*—I read somewhere that you said that *Real Italian Pizza* was your first dramatic film. I'm wondering if, well, you may not stick by that anymore, but would you say that *Canadian Pacific I* and *II* were dramatic films?

Rimmer: What does "dramatic" mean? I mean, sure.

MacKenzie: I guess I'm interested in exploring that question. What does dramatic mean and how does that play into your work more generally?

Rimmer: Whew! I don't know.

MacKenzie: Obviously there's not an apparent narrative going on there, but time is passing. There's a beginning, a middle and an end, and things do occur that are . . .

Rimmer: There's one person in it.

MacKenzie: Yeah, and there's potential drama. Some could say, you know, Michael Snow's *Wavelength* is a dramatic film.

Rimmer: Well, he has actual actors who do things.

MacKenzie: Yeah, things happen there, yeah.

Rimmer: I don't know.

MacKenzie: Would you say that you've ever had any resistance to drama?

Rimmer: I've never done it consciously.

MacKenzie: I am wondering about *Fracture*?

Rimmer: Well, you could say that is my first dramatic film, I guess. There's a man and a woman and a child, and they do things, you know, and you can read things through it.

MacKenzie: The presence of individuals, of people and their

interaction. The bit I read mentioned that, and said it seems to stem from an interest in that dramatic modality you claimed in *Real Italian Pizza*, and it works with a limited number of shots to kind of invent drama where maybe it didn't even exist. It's actually one of my favourite pieces by you.

Rimmer: *Fracture*. Yeah, they were separate . . . separate . . . images. They weren't in the same space at all.

MacKenzie: Yeah, yeah, so you were kind of inventing a drama there.

Rimmer: Yeah.

MacKenzie: Located in the realm of, obviously, the nuclear family and gender, generational, maybe civilizing tension.

Rimmer: Yeah, You can read it that way. I remember people— academics reading it like that, "Oh! This is the Oedipal family. This is the da da da . . ."

MacKenzie: I think especially from your past work there is a sense of—wow! This is the first time we're seeing actors. Well, obviously not actors, but people moving through space and . . . What inspired that shift? What got you . . .

Rimmer: I don't know, probably Kuleshov. That idea.

MacKenzie: Was it in the editing process, or seeing the way we react to the placing of . . .

Rimmer: Yeah, just trying to, you know, piece together two different things and make a narrative. Make it seem that it's the same thing, you know, whereas it's not.

MacKenzie: It seems—to me it seemed like an extension of the looping exploration as well because we're repeating, but we're moving things around. But it seems to be changing with this film. Would you . . . ?

Rimmer: It repeats. It has a kind of mathematically figured out structure, somewhat, as I remember. I don't know, it was a long time ago. It's hard to remember why you did things because often you do them . . . I often rely on instinct. Is it instinct? Yeah. Something feels like it's working, I'll go for it without questioning it too much.

MacKenzie: Do you find you can get a clear space all the time to find that—to believe your instinct, I guess would be the question. Or do you, think, "Oh, I'm bogged down with a bunch of whatever is going on in my life at the time," or, "I'm rushed," or, you know? Are you able to find that instinct pretty regularly?

Rimmer: Well, I know if something's working or not.

MacKenzie: Yeah, regardless.

Rimmer: I don't know necessarily why. It's easy to say why it's not working but when it is it's a bit more difficult. You recognize there's something happening there.

MacKenzie: And working—

Rimmer: And potential for something interesting to come out, to be read into it.

» » »

MacKenzie: You've already talked a bit about this, but your use of loops and looping, and how you think maybe repetition and cycling can work, and to what progressive effect: can you talk a bit about that? How it changes as you're watching?

Rimmer: I think I've found that if you loop something, you look at something over and over and over and over and over again, it starts to take on a different meaning than just seeing it once. And as I was saying before, I like to look at these things over and over until they start to speak back to me. And the loop, you know, there's all sorts of metaphors that go with looping, you know. Trapped somewhere, can't get out of it, in a rut. Sort of stuff. And other more positive interpretations, I guess. [...]

MacKenzie: When you're working on that looping cycle are you . . . do you find yourself sitting there watching it and thinking, "Okay enough. This is long enough"?

Rimmer: Yeah. Yeah.

MacKenzie: That there's been a transformation?

Rimmer: See, you've got to do something to it, or there's got to be an ending, or there's got to be something, unless it's just a projection, you know, an environment—then it can go on forever. But *Seashore* was an experiment in contact printing. When I was living in New York then and I got to know a guy called Stan Lawder, who is an experimental filmmaker—you might know his work—and he had built a contact printer out of an old camera or projector, I can't remember what. So I made that film, I had some stock footage of people at the seashore bathing . . . and we passed this through his contact printer over and over again in different ways, and we would do things even, like, as the film was going through the contact printer, physically grab onto the film and hold it back so it would rip the sprockets out—and the film would start going funny ways. So that was like getting physically involved, really physically getting involved with the film to the extent of actually destroying it.

MacKenzie: Right. So yeah, a different, a pretty different process than watching the loop. It's like you're laying that loop down and manipulating it.

Rimmer: Yeah. Disrespectfully too, you know, by letting it rip itself apart.

» » »

MacKenzie: At that time you were doing these optical effects, whose equipment were you using to achieve those effects? Where were you going to do that?

Rimmer: I built my own optical printer.

MacKenzie: Okay.

Rimmer: When I lived in New York. And they were very simple to build then. You needed a Bolex and you need an old projector and then a light bulb. Or I did a lot of—which I found was easier and more interesting—was to shoot, not to do optical printing at all but to do re-photography where you're shooting off a screen, a rear screen or a front screen. *Cellophane Wrapper* is all re-photography. There's no optical printing in that sense.

MacKenzie: And then manipulations at the lab level in terms of colourization, or?

Rimmer: No, I would usually do it—when I was copying off the wall, I would use filters, colour filters, just stick them in front of the camera or in front of the projector. Like, *Cellophane Wrapper* involved projecting—two projectors—one containing a negative image and one containing a positive image of the same thing, but not synchronized.

MacKenzie: Right.

Rimmer: And projected onto a screen.

MacKenzie: A single screen.

Rimmer: Right. And lined up. And that allowed me to put colour filters over the negative or over the positive and get colour separations. That kind of thing.

MacKenzie: And so, I mean, that's a particular approach to film-making, and strategy, you know. Technically and physically there's a particular thing going on there in terms of how you achieve that. Is the material—the shape of the film-determined in some way by the availability of these things for you in any given film? […] If you've got an idea with this loop, are you thinking, "Okay, I'm going to apply this technology to it so I can achieve this thing that's in my head"? Or are you thinking, "This technology might, might . . ."

Rimmer: I just start working with it and see where it leads me, rather than as I said before, coming in with a preconceived idea of where it's going to go.

MacKenzie: So you're playing with—

Rimmer: Like *Cellophane Wrapper*. I didn't think, "Oh, this is a film about feminism, and it's about women stuck in a factory. How am I going to do that?" No. That came . . . that meaning came way after I even made the film. I mean, I always think it's really important to listen to your images, to watch them and let them tell you what they're about rather than imposing. When you start imposing it becomes really didactic.

MacKenzie: And no fun.

Rimmer: Theoretical and deadly.

MacKenzie: And so coming away from the sort of strategy you took to make that film . . . maybe strategy is not really a good word—but the sort of manner that it ended up being made, do you then move onto your next film and think, "This worked last time, maybe I can incorporate this technique or methodology into this"? Or is it strictly based on source material, and like you said before, working with the material and just coming up with something as you move along?

Rimmer: Well, I might use the same technique. I mean, the same technique of re-photography. Sure. Because I know how to do that.

MacKenzie: Right. And you've finessed it somewhat, maybe.

Rimmer: Yeah. And I might do it a little differently. Like *Surfacing on the Thames*, which was another early film I made at the same time as *Cellophane*, is re-photography. But it's using a modified slide projector instead of a film camera—or film projector. And I'm still—you know, when I'm using images, even in the work I'm doing now, I'll often shoot those images off a Steenbeck, for example, rather than using conventional printing techniques. Because I know how to do that; I know how to control things, and I can get a lot more variables in there by doing that than I can with traditional, say, optical printing.

MacKenzie: Yeah, yeah. It's interesting because some would say, "Well, you're going to lose some quality there but what you . . . "

Rimmer: No, you gain something else.

» » »

MacKenzie: It's interesting. It makes me think of how many wannabe filmmakers I know who aren't doing things because they claim they're limited by technical setbacks or, "I can't do this because I don't have the ability to: x, y, z." Whereas I see what you're doing and nothing's getting in the way, and—

Rimmer: You just figure out a way to do it.

MacKenzie: Yeah, and that—potentially, you know, bad situations have silver linings and you can find something in them, or . . .

Rimmer: Like doing re-photography instead of optical printing because optical printing is really tricky, you know.

MacKenzie: It's a pain in the ass.

Rimmer: [*Gesturing*] A frame at a time.

MacKenzie: Yeah, I hate being in those dark rooms.

Rimmer: Projecting onto a small screen and re-shooting it is a lot faster but it also allows you to do things you can't do with optical printing. You're working with flicker patterns which you don't get with optical printing, right? With *Cellophane Wrapper* I couldn't have done that the same way with an optical printer because I was playing with the flicker. I had three machines going—two projectors all going off and on at different times, and the camera all going off and on, so there's three rhythms going there. So if you look at the strip of film they might see the negative image for a couple of frames and then a frame of positive and then a couple of frames of black where it was in its off-phase.

MacKenzie: I have actually looked at it that way.

Rimmer: And by changing the speed of the various machines you get different rhythms going.

MacKenzie: Were you ever working with variable speed projectors when you were doing this sort of stuff?

Rimmer: Well I put a Rheostat on my projector so I could slow it down and speed it up.

MacKenzie: Without burning.

Rimmer: Yeah, I knew where the edge was, where it would start to burn. But I use burns. In *Migration*—a burning image and burning frame.

» » »

MacKenzie: Do you feel like that handling of the film is crucial to your practice?

Rimmer: Oh yeah.

MacKenzie: Even if you end up on video?

Rimmer: Oh yeah. Yeah, because I am handling it. When I've finished working, my hands are covered with blue ink. I'm physically holding and scratching and painting.

MacKenzie: I've seen some of that material. I've been in the room at the NFB where you were working. I think you were out of town and we did a little film shoot in there and there's some great material there, hanging everywhere.

Rimmer: Right. Yeah, I've been fortunate that the Film Board has given me a room to work in to do this stuff, which is great. It's their old 35mm Steenbeck room, but nobody's using 35 anymore except me so I have this room. I'm just keeping my fingers crossed that it'll continue and they won't want to move some computers in there at some point in time. So I'm able to do the actual painting there and make a mess, and then I do the editing at home on a computer.

» » »

MacKenzie: How do you feel about different approaches to viewing your work in general? I mean, there's the gallery setting, there's the rear cinema setting . . .

Rimmer: Well, *Landscape*, as you said, *Landscape* was also shown in a gallery rear-projected onto a false wall, as was *Canadian Pacific*. It was done in a gallery too, rear film projections, not video, rear film projections. The stuff I'm doing now is hand painting on film, I'm showing in different ways also. One way is it exists as a film, or a video. A beginning, and an end, the credits, a score. It can also exist as an installation in a gallery. Maybe three monitors, different things going on, different loops. But I've also been using that material and showing it at dance parties and working with DJs . . . and that's been really interesting, sort of penetrating into that world of dance, DJ, etcetera. And it seems to work, that stuff, very well in that context and people really are interested. They've never seen this sort of stuff before. A lot of the stuff you see in rave parties, dance parties, is computer graphics, which can be pretty boring.

MacKenzie: Yeah, I'd say the bulk is computer graphics or found footage, maybe . . .

Rimmer: Or found footage that just kind of runs by for no reason.

MacKenzie: So you're doing live switching in those situations?

Rimmer: Sometimes. Sometimes I'll just maybe have a VHS and a DVD player, and I can get one going and then switch to the other one. Sometimes I can switch back and forth through a switch, depending on what equipment they have.

MacKenzie: So you're flexible with whatever their stuff might entail.

Rimmer: Yeah.

MacKenzie: And do you feel like when you're doing that you may be working through ideas? Is it a process in that way, in terms of what the final thing might look like, or . . . ?

Rimmer: I'll often use stuff that I'm working on, and that will give me an idea of how it's working, how it's holding up, you know—watching it as hours and hours go by.

MacKenzie: Not so different than looking at those loops back in the day.

Rimmer: Yeah. Yeah, sort of testing it out, seeing how it works, and then getting feedback from people too, like, "Wow man, how'd you do that? What program did you use?" But I'm using a Steenbeck. And those films are quite interesting because they're combining three different mediums. There's painting, because I am painting on film, and I'm learning about paint and inks and chemicals. Film because it's on 35 mm film. And digital video because I'm copying off the Steenbeck with a digital video camera and then doing some manipulation in the editing, not a lot, but some. More and more actually now.

» » »

MacKenzie: *Al Neil: A Portait* and *Jack Wise: Language of the Brush* are in tandem. Do you want to talk about that a bit? How they . . .

Rimmer: What were you going to ask me about *Al*?

MacKenzie: Well, I was going to ask you—well, I was going to say, as far as I know that was your first long piece.

Rimmer: I think so, yeah.

MacKenzie: Though I guess there had been some dance documentations stuff, but this is more formally your first long piece that amalgamated a lot of preoccupations of your earlier work and brought them together in a way. I wanted to ask you about the changes involved in that shift and how those came together. Was it again that instinctual working from your gut? Shooting a bunch of material and then just playing?

Rimmer: Well, it was a desire to make a film with Al, because Al

AL NEIL, A PORTRAIT, 1979

is an important person on the scene and he had some influence on . . .

MacKenzie: How well did you know him at that time?

Rimmer: Not very well when I first started. I got to know him in the process.

MacKenzie: Right. That must have played in a bit to the making of the film as well.

Rimmer: Yeah.

MacKenzie: Your relationship.

Rimmer: Yeah, we got to know each other.

MacKenzie: Did you consciously choose this to be your first long-form work or did it just happen?

Rimmer: It just happened. I needed that length, I guess. Forty minutes, is it? Something like that?

MacKenzie: Yeah. But you were going to talk about Jack Wise and Al Neil.

Rimmer: Well, Jack Wise is a painter. Do you know his work at all?

MacKenzie: Yeah.

Rimmer: He was very interested in Eastern painting and calligraphic painting and Tibetan Mandala painting. And I first met him in the sixties when I was just beginning as a filmmaker and he was sort of beginning. Although he was older than me, he was sort of beginning his painting career. And right from that point, really interested in particularly Tibetan ways of painting. And we talked about, you know, "Why don't we do a film together some day? Yeah, okay." And I'd run into him like five years later because he'd moved out of town. He was up on Denman and various other islands and we'd say, "Hey, are you still interested? Yeah. Yeah. Give me a call. Yeah." And we didn't do anything. Didn't do anything. And then he phoned me up . . . I guess this was seven or eight years ago. He said, "Are you still interested?" And I said, "Yeah." And he said, "Well, you better hurry because I'm pretty sick and I'm not going to make it through the winter." And I said, "Okay, I'll head up." And there was no time to get money, and I borrowed an early version of a DV camera from the Film Board, and I was living on a boat at that time in Coal Harbour, and Sarah and I took off up to Denman Island on the boat. Got just off Bowen Island and the rudder broke, and I managed to limp back to Vancouver—to Coal Harbour.

MacKenzie: That's a whole story there, isn't it?

JACK WISE, LANGUAGE OF THE BRUSH, 1998

Rimmer: Yeah. And phoned up Jack, said, "Jack, sorry I didn't make it, got rudder problems." And typical Jack, he quoted the *I Ching*. He said, "Difficulty in the beginning and sure of success in the future. Try again." So got the rudder fixed and went back up. And he was pretty weak. He was sleeping a lot, and still working on his little, very small things. So we shot for about four days of him talking, of him doing these things. The landscape that he was living is in some of his paintings.

MacKenzie: And it was just the three of you? Sarah was living there as well, or?

Rimmer: Just Sarah and I and him, and the woman who he was living with then, whose name I can't remember. Barbara, I think her name was. And then I took that material and I rough cut it, and I went to the Film Board to see if I could get some money, and ran into Gillian Darling there, who's a producer there at that time, and she really liked [my] stuff. And after some consultation she said, "Why, y'know, we could make this a full Film Board production." Which means you give up all rights to it but you get paid well. So I did that. So they gave me some money and I went over to—by this time Jack had died. I went to the Victoria Art Gallery which had a huge collection of his work. In fact, he'd given all his work to them when he died. So I went up and shot on 16mm as much of his work as I could. And then cut that together.

MacKenzie: Tableau-style or moving around a bit, or?

Rimmer: No, just head-on stuff. And what I wanted to do was not just do kind of a straight documentary on him but engage in a kind of visual conversation so that I was creating images with my camera by going out into nature the same as he was going out into nature or into his head and creating images, so I wanted a dialogue of images rather than words. And his connection with Al Neil—Al Neil as you know is a legend, he's still alive, a legendary bebop jazz musician—ex-junkie, assemblist, collagist, writer, performer . . . and both Jack and Al, I realized, were both sort of looking for the same thing. They were both looking for some kind of spiritual connection or meaning to life—Jack through discipline, through meditation, through yoga, through studying the ancient texts—Al through excess, you know, which is another avenue. You just do everything you can and take everything you can and mess your mind up and see where it leads. So I sometimes show both those films together—not side-by-side at the same time, but one after the other.

» » »

MacKenzie: *Black Cat White Cat* and *Local Knowledge*. I'll just talk about—for me both of these films seem to have an epic quality to them. There's a sense that they're covering a lot of material. They're really mature works that are—they cover vast expanses of inner and outer territories. Was there a conscious choice on your part that you wanted to get at these very broad, and—

Rimmer: Well, with *Local Knowledge*, yeah. I was trying to investigate different levels of consciousness. I mean, there's the ocean which figures predominately, and there's what's going on above the ocean and below the ocean, so you can think of it as levels of consciousness or unconscious, things coming up from the unconscious, etcetera. I don't want to talk about it too much.

MacKenzie: Yeah.

Rimmer: But, yeah, that was definitely in the works there, which is about the kind of subject matter that I'm dealing with in the new film that I'm making, which I won't talk much about.

MacKenzie: You won't?

Rimmer: No. It's too early to—and especially attaching those kind of labels to it. *Black Cat White Cat* was much more, much simpler I think. It's really just what I saw in China.

MacKenzie: Subject-based, yeah.

Rimmer: Images that I saw that I thought were interesting and would work together. And the interesting thing about *Black Cat White Cat* is that it was made when I took my students to China. It was six months before Tiananmen Square happened. And I had shot the film—I had edited it pretty quickly, and I was showing it at the Toronto Experimental Film Festival . . .

MacKenzie: The Images Festival.

Rimmer: Or one of them. I can't remember which one it was. So I showed it in the daytime in my screening. Came back to the hotel that evening, turned on the TV and there was Tiananmen Square happening on the TV, and I thought, "Oh fuck! This changes my whole film." Y'know, I thought, "Well, how can I acknowledge this?" Because probably a lot of the students who we had met in China at the Beijing Film Academy were there in Tiananmen Square and they may have been killed, you know, and I thought, "Gee, I've got to do something to acknowledge," otherwise it's kind of an empty, just a visual documentary and, "What'll I do? What'll I do? I don't know." So I went outside and there was a protest march going by the hotel up to the Chinese Consulate, and a man came up, a young man, and he handed me a piece of paper, and I read it and it said, "Last communiqué from Beijing Radio." And it was a one sheet about—telling people what had happened in Tiananmen Square. Tanks had come in and run over our people, and da da da da da. And the last thing it said, "Due to unusual circumstances here in Beijing this is the last communiqué we can make." So I thought, "That's it! That's the text." So I put that at the end of the film. Had to re-cut a little bit. I think I coloured it red, white on red or something. Put some tank sounds underneath it, and when the film ends that thing comes up. And that's that text that announces what was going on. So it puts it in another context.

MacKenzie: Just forces you to turn your head in a way that it wouldn't have otherwise.

Rimmer: But it's not complex in the way that *Local Knowledge* is. It's pretty well all . . . Although we had a lot of fun playing with it, with the sound; there's a lot of sound in *Black Cat White Cat* that I picked up off the radio in China. English language lessons which I found very humorous because they have these lessons and they need some kind of story, you know, to learn the language. So they would come up with these absolutely absurd stories about meeting—Who was it on the bus? John Denver.

MacKenzie: What role does sound play in your work in terms of process? Is it something that comes afterwards, or?

Rimmer: It often comes afterwards. A lot of film, early films didn't have any sound deliberately. I didn't want any sound. But I've been working—I guess seven or eight or maybe more films I've worked with Dennis Burke as composer and sound designer. And I think the China film was the first one we did together. And we've got to the point now where we understand each other pretty well so I don't have to talk a lot about it. I show him the stuff and say, "Dennis, da da da da da," and he will come up with something really quickly. So it's a comfortable creative relationship there. So I have certain ideas about it but I give him lots of room—to come up with something.

» » »

Rimmer: [. . .] I've made films in Europe, I mean, I made a couple of films in Eastern Europe, one which you probably have never seen, called *Perestroyka* (1992).

MacKenzie: Yeah, I know of it but I haven't seen it.

Rimmer: Which I made in Russia. A documentary about what's going on in the arts in Russia during the change of ideology, etcetera. And I made a feature documentary in Poland on— have you seen that one, called *Under the Lizards* (1994)?

MacKenzie: No. I haven't.

Rimmer: It's about jazz in Poland. It's about the role that jazz music played in the political situation in Eastern Europe with—jazz was really the first form of political protest in Eastern Europe, the playing of American jazz, you know, which was outlawed by the communist authorities.

MacKenzie: And those two works were built of some time spent there, and so again, you turn your camera on and start filming things because you're there and you're inspired?

Rimmer: Yeah.

MacKenzie: Not necessarily like, "I'm going there to make a film about"?

Rimmer: Well, I'd gone to Poland a few—I'd had a show in . . . I was invited to a show in Hungary, and this was just when things were changing—perestroika and whatnot—and met some people from Poland, so I went on to Poland, and I

UNDER THE LIZARDS, 1994

showed in the art schools in Poland. And I loved it, and I went back again. I took my students to Poland for a field trip—we visited film schools. And I remember sitting in a bar in Kraków with Dennis Burke, who's a long-time collaborator, sound designer, and composer, and he was one of the other teachers on this trip with the students, and we said, "Jeez, we've got to get back here somehow, you know, this is really interesting." We just loved Poland. We said, "How are we going to do it? Let's make a film, of course, but what are we going to make it on?" And we'd been hanging out in jazz clubs in Kraków and Warsaw, and meeting jazz musicians because Dennis is a musician as well as being a sound designer. And we decided, "Let's make a film about jazz, that'll be the doorway in." You know, there could have been other doorways, but that seemed to be an interesting doorway. So we did. And we hustled up some money, and we got a little crew together, and we went, and we stayed six weeks in Poland shooting jazz concerts, even classical concerts, punk concerts, talking to people. And that ended up as a feature length documentary which is somewhat different than I usually do, although I used a lot of my experimental techniques, some re-photography, certainly in the cutting it was more—kind of more interpretive than a normal documentary. When I work in documentary I like to think of it more as poetic documentary, you know, where I'm not really trying to hammer something home. I'm kind of looking and seeing what I see and trying to make sense of it through visuals.

MacKenzie: And do you feel the same liberty and freedom as you do with your other kinds of work when you're doing that?

Rimmer: Yeah. Yeah, it's a different thing but, yeah, I mean, I do what I want to do. You know, like, with the Poland film I was fortunate to get enough funding—because it was quite— through Canada Council, even through BC Film. One of the first times I've ever tried that, and I got some money from them. That was interesting in one way: that we shot in video, we shot with very high-end, Hi-8 cameras, the industrial Hi-8 cameras, came back to Vancouver, transferred it to film from video, which is the wrong way to do it, through the Film Board. They came in and they transferred all this stuff, then I cut on film and ended up with a film which was— combined—there was some film, actual film in it, but it was mostly ninety percent video. And it looked great. I was really pleased with it.

» » »

MacKenzie: So, I think I'm just going to ask you a little bit about the various geographical spaces you've worked in, starting with Vancouver.

Rimmer: Okay.

MacKenzie: So, you've been in Vancouver for a long time. Are you from Vancouver?

Rimmer: Yeah, I was born here.

MacKenzie: Okay. And it's changed a lot as a city, in probably the— well, definitely in the time you've lived here. What do you think of your relationship is to this city? How would you express that? I'm going to ask it in a bunch of different ways, so you can take your pick. What does Vancouver mean to you relative to your work, I guess, and as a geographical space, as a social space, as a community space?

Rimmer: Mmm.

MacKenzie: I mean, you're still here, there must be a reason.

Rimmer: Yeah, I go away. I mean, I travel, but . . .

MacKenzie: Yeah, I think for a lot of people it's a destination. A lot of people come here from elsewhere is my experience of it, and a lot of people leave. They come briefly and then they disappear again. There's definitely something about this city that prompts that, more so, I'd say, than other cities. Do you have any kind of perspective on this city and how it's influenced or impacted on you?

Rimmer: Well, the landscape of the city, or the countryside, figures pretty predominately in a lot of my films. I was thinking the other day that probably over half of my films contain images of water—of the sea. And I grew up on the ocean. I grew up in West Van before it was "West Van," and we lived right on the beach. So I grew up swimming and fishing and watching the sea and collecting driftwood and hiking in the forest and so that's sort of really ingrained in me. So this is really where I want to be.

MacKenzie: Right.

Rimmer: Although I may go again and live somewhere else for a while.

MacKenzie: Mm hmm. But there's a historical attachment.

Rimmer: Yeah.

MacKenzie: At the very least.

Rimmer: Oh yeah. Yeah.

MacKenzie: And obviously, I mean, when you lived in New York, for example, *Real Italian Pizza* was something that you shot out of your loft window, and so you were working with your environment in that case.

Rimmer: Mmm hmm.

MacKenzie: And, like you say, water [is] so predominant in some of your works. Obviously your landscape is having an impact on you here in Vancouver. Do you think you would miss that if you were somewhere else and not able to make the kind of works you want to make, or would you adapt?

Rimmer: Well, I missed it when I lived in New York. I mean, I loved living in New York, it was really exciting, but I did miss the sea and I missed the mountains and I missed the forest and the natural world. So, we would come back actually every summer from New York.

MacKenzie: Did you miss the rain?

Rimmer: I missed the rain even, yeah. And generally we'd come back and go straight up the coast to Storm Bay. It's a place that—a piece of property that I'm involved in with a group of people; we bought it in, I guess, the late sixties.

MacKenzie: As a group?

Rimmer: As a group. We were—at that time we were university students, or some activists and drug dealers, you know, a mix of people. I mean, I have a very strong tie to that particular landscape. A lot of the images that you see in a film like *Local Knowledge* were shot at Storm Bay. Trying to work with the rhythms of nature there, with the wind and the tide and the sun. Did a lot of time-lapse work there. And things like setting my camera up on my boat at anchor, and with a time-lapse device on the camera, allowing the wind and the tide to move the boat back and forth at anchor, and single framing as it did that. *Narrows Inlet* is one example of that too.

» » »

MacKenzie: How do you imagine the future of the avant-garde?

Rimmer: I think the boundaries are just getting blurred now. I mean, I don't consider myself an avant-garde filmmaker anymore, I mean, I'm just a filmmaker. I mean, you can see, you know, you go on the Internet and you can see thousands of experimental films. Everybody's making them, it's very easy to do. So, I'm just a filmmaker now. Now I'm working in animation. I've done experimental; I've done dance film; I've done documentary; I've done portraits of artists; and now I'm moving onto my form of animation which involves hand painting, clear 35mm.

MacKenzie: So, it's all one big media.

Rimmer: Yeah.

MacKenzie: And do you think that, that blurring of the boundaries is a good thing?

Rimmer: Oh yeah.

MacKenzie: Is it helpful?

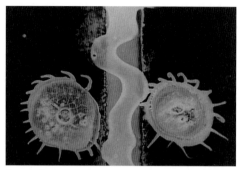

DIGITAL PSYCHE, 2008

Rimmer: Sure.

MacKenzie: There's no sense that the value, maybe, is reduced because there's so much of it? Or that it's easier, as you say, anyone can do it, it's easier? I'm curious because I think— you're right, there is a lot of it out there and, I mean, there's a lot that's terrible too. The more there is, the more awful stuff there is too. But does that material carry any weight? Or is it fleeting and ephemeral in a way that, that, you know—when you were doing your initial work that stuff wasn't; it was front and centre. Do you think that change is . . . ?

Rimmer: Well, people now are much more willing to accept film that breaks rules. Anything goes now and that has a lot to do with the Internet and with people kind of being empowered in knowing that they can just get a camera and do something. It may be shitty but they can do it, you know, and some people are coming out with wonderful things. People are making political documentaries for nothing now. You've seen wonderful stuff coming out—a lot of bad stuff—but people are not as intimidated as they were. You can make something. To work in 16mm film is prohibitive now for most people.

MacKenzie: And it was prohibitive just in terms of the accessibility. And the mind set of, "This is something that you need to know a lot about before you can touch it." Whereas now it's like, "Pick up a camera." It's not nearly as complicated. And so that access to the masses, the so-called masses, means that there's more of it, and it's more available, and like you say, less intimidating. So, that language that's been built out of the kind of work that you made earlier in your career is available to everybody now. But do you think that people are actually breaking ground in the same way that the ground had been broken back in the day?

Rimmer: They are breaking more new ground in documentary, I think. You know, we're seeing documentaries that are really critical and that have an impact.

MacKenzie: So it may be that the groundbreaking has less to do with strategy and technique and more to do with politics and being able to get to an audience, speaking to an audience.

Rimmer: Mm hmm.

MacKenzie: What advice would you give to artists working in media today? It seems you're saying they have less barriers than you did, but at the same time maybe they're completely immersed in this language from the moment they're born and so it might be hard to see past it. I think you were looking around and saying, "Hey, there are many things we could do here that haven't been done," and now I think kids grow up and go, "Oh my God there's—"

Rimmer: "Everything's been done."

MacKenzie: It feels like everything's been done, "What do I do?"

Rimmer: Well, make it new. Who was the poet that said that? Was it Pound or somebody like that? You know, you've got to make it new every time. It's the same old stories. Make them new, make them fresh. Another slant on it. And don't be afraid to do anything, really.

MacKenzie: Do you think people are more afraid now than they were back in the sixties and seventies?

Rimmer: No.

MacKenzie: They're less afraid?

Rimmer: Less afraid, yeah, because they can do it. They can take one of these little cameras and do it, you know, and make something. If they have some intelligence they can make something and the audience is not turned off by it.

Transcribed by Josh Byer and Anne Scheid.

DAVID RIMMER

Filmography

2008 *Digital Psyche*
      12 mins, video

2006 *Padayatra (Walking Meditation)*
      12 mins, video

2003 *An Eye for an Eye*
      12 mins, video
      On the Road to Kandahar
      5 mins, video

2002 *Early Hand-Painted Series*
      30 mins, video
          Axis Mundi, 4.5 mins
          Lost in the Forest, 4 mins
          Sleight of Hand, 3.5 mins
          Moon Blind, 3.5 mins
          Fish Scales for Stan Brakhage, 3 mins
          Playing the Scales, 3 mins
          Looks Like Rain, 45 secs
          Diamonds are a Girl's Best Friend, 3 mins
          Membrane, 3.5 mins
          Tide Pool, 3.5 mins

1999 *Traces of Emily Carr*
      30 mins, Beta SP

1998 *Jack Wise: Language of the Brush*
      45 mins, 16mm

1997 *Codes of Conduct*
      9 mins, 16mm

1994 *Tiger*
      5 mins, 35mm
      Under the Lizards
      77 mins, 16mm

1992 *Local Knowledge*
      30 mins, 16mm
      Perestroyka
      60 mins, video
      Beaubourg Boogie Woogie
      5 mins, 16mm

1989 *Black Cat White Cat It's a Good Cat if It Catches the Mouse*
      35 mins, 16mm
      Divine Mannequin
      7 mins, video to film transfer

1988 *Roadshow*
      20 mins, Betacam

1986 *Along the Road to Altimira*
      18 mins, 16mm
      As Seen on TV
      14 mins, 16mm

1984 *Bricolage*
      11 mins, 16mm
      Sisyphus
      20 mins, video

1982 *Shades of Red*
      40 mins, 16mm

1980 *Narrows Inlet*
      8 mins, 16mm

1979 *Al Neil: A Portrait*
      40 mins, 16mm

1975 *Canadian Pacific II*
      10 mins, 16mm

1974 *Canadian Pacific I*
      10 mins, 16mm

1973 *Watching for the Queen*
      10 mins, 16mm Silent
      Fracture
      10 mins, 16 mm Silent

1971 *Seashore*
      10 mins, 16mm Silent
      Real Italian Pizza
      10 mins, 16mm

1970   *The Dance*
     5 mins, 16mm
     Surfacing on the Thames
     10 mins, 16mm
     Variations on a Cellophane Wrapper
     8 mins, 16mm
     Treefall
     5 mins, 16mm
     Blue Movie
     5 mins, 16mm

1969   *Migration*
     10 mins, 16mm

1968   *Square Inch Field*
     10 mins, 16mm

1967   *West Coast* (1967-present)
     30 mins – 2 hours + (various releases)
     Knowplace
     11 mins, 16mm
     Head/End
     2 mins, 16mm

VIDEOGRAPHY

2008 *Digital Psyche*
12 mins

2005 *Padayatra (Walking Meditation)*
12 mins

2003 *On the Road to Kandahar*
5 mins
An Eye for an Eye
12 mins

2002 *Early Hand Painted Series*
30 mins

1999 *Traces of Emily Carr*
30 mins

1992 *Perestroyka*
85 mins

1989 *Divine Mannequin*
Video Installation and Film.

1987 *Road Show*
21 mins

1986 *Steal the Thunder*
10 mins
As Seen on TV
14 min, also on film.

1984 *Sisyphus*
        22 mins

1983 *Solo from Chaos*
        10 mins
        Bach Duet
        8 mins
        Two-monitor piece

1978 *Hello*
        7 mins

1975 *Show Of Numbers*
        Video installation
        Box Cars
        4 mins

Bibliography

1968

Reif, Tony. "Letter from Vancouver." *Take One* 2.2 (Nov-Dec 1968): 26.

1969

Schroeder, Andreas. "Movies: Producers Rate Top Honors." *Province* (Vancouver) 12 September 1969: 33.

Townsend, Charlotte. "And the Camera Betrays the Hand and Eye." *Vancouver Sun* 12 September 1969: 29.

1970

Daniels, Edgar. "The Ann Arbor Film Festival: An Applause of Films." *New Cinema Review* 1.3 (1970): 20-26.

Paquet, Andre. "Qu'est-ce que le cinéma canadien?" Trans. P. Jacques. *Artscanada* 142-143 (April 1970): 3-6.

Schroeder, Andreas. "Films: Simple Genius." *Province*. (Vancouver) 31 July 1970: 6.

Tougas, Kirk. "Vancouver Letter." *Take One* 2.11 (May-June 1970): 29.

Youngblood, Gene. "The New Canadian Cinema: Images from the Age of Paradox." *Artscanada* 142-143 (April 1970): 7-13.

1971

Curtis, David. "Opticals—Film as Film and Found Footage." In *Experimental Cinema: A Fifty Year Evolution*. New York: Dell Publishing Co. Inc., 1971. 140-46.

"David Rimmer." In *Filmmakers' Series* No. 30, *Canyon Cinema News* 3 (1971): 4.

1972

Gilbert, Gerry. "An Evening of Dave Rimmer's Films." In *Form and Structure in Recent Film*. Ed. Dennis Wheeler. Exhibition Catalogue. Vancouver: Vancouver Art Gallery and Talonbooks, 1972. n.pag.

Greenspun, Roger. "The Dance: The Films of David Rimmer." *New York Times* 26 February 1972: 18.

———. "Quick—Who Are David Rimmer and James Herbert?" *New York Times* 8 October 1972: sec. 2, p. 17.

"In View." *Art and Artists* 7.9 (December 1972): 8-9.

Le Grice, Malcolm. "Thoughts on Recent Underground Film." *Afterimage* (London) 4 (Autumn 1972): 78-95.

Melnyk, L. "Experimental Films … 'The Flawless Pattern of Rotation.'" *Queen's Journal* (Kingston) 29 September 1972: 8.

Moritz, William. "Film Books: Three Books on Experimental Cinema." *Film Quarterly* 25.4 (Summer 1972): 31-34.

Nordstrom, Kristina. "Film: Celebrations of Life and Death." *Village Voice* (New York) 6 April 1972: 79.

———. "The Films of David Rimmer." *Film Library Quarterly*
5.2 (Summer 1972): 28-31, 41.

1973

DuCane, John. "The Festival of Light and Time Continues."
Time Out 7 (September 1973).

"Exhibition of Contemporary Canadian Art to Be Held in
Paris." *Cinema Canada*, 2nd ser., no. 8 (June-July 1973): 9.

Klepac, Walter. "Art: Films by David Rimmer." *Guerilla* 3.24
(March 1973): M2.

Koller, Georg Csaba. "Filmpeople, Filmpeople, Filmpeople."
Cinema Canada, 2nd ser., no. 7 (April-May 1973): 15.

Le Grice, Malcolm. "Vision." *Studio International* 185.952
(February 1973): 52.

———. "Vision." *Studio International* 185.953 (March 1973):
104.

Nicolson, Annabel. "Canadada Fragments." *Art and Artists* 8.1
(April 1973): 28-33.

Paquet, Andre. "Cinéastes: Les espaces visuels ou les savants du
24 images seconde." *Canada Trajectories* 73. Exhibition
Catalogue. Montreal: Editions Mediart, 1973: n. pag.

———. "Cinéma expérimental: Les espaces visuals ou les
savants du 24 images seconde." *Cinéma Québec* 3.1
(September 1973): 33-35.

1974

"David Rimmer." *Personal Film: Content and Context*. Ed. Tony
Rief and Kirk Tougas. Vancouver: Intermedia Press, 1974.

Edwards, Natalie. "Moving Art." *Cinema Canada*, 2nd ser., no. 13
(April-May 1974): 54-55.

Freyer, Ellen. "Formalist Cinema: Artistic Suicide in the Avant-
Garde." *Velvet Light Trap* 13 (Fall 1974): 47-49.

Gale, Peggy. "The National Gallery's Canadian Filmmakers
Series: Canadian Artists as Filmmakers." *Artmagazine* 6.19
(Fall 1974): 28.

Hancox, Rick. "Short Films." *Cinema Canada*, 2nd ser., no. 14
(June-July 1974): 58-60.

Ibranyi-Kiss, A. "Filmmaking West Coast Style: Jack Darcus."
Cinema Canada, 2nd ser., no. 13 (April-May 1974): 42-45.

1976

Edwards, Natalie. "It's Film All Right, but is It Art?" *Cinema
Canada,* 3rd ser., no. 26 (March 1976): 18-20.

Eizykan, Claudine. "La distribution des écarts." in *La jouissance
—cinéma*. Paris: Union Générale d'Éditions, 1976. 292-96.

Gould, Michael. "The Artist-Inventor." In *Surrealism and the
Cinema*. London: Tantivy, 1976.

1977

Beattie, Eleanor. "Rimmer, David." In *A Handbook of Canadian Film*. 2d ed. Toronto: Peter Martin Associates, 1977. 163-4.

Birnie, Ian, Tony Reif, and Jean-Pierre Bastien. "Independent Views." *Cinema Canada* no. 38-39 (June-July 1977): 45-49.

Ibranyi-Kiss, A. "Filmmaking West Coast Style: Jack Darcus." In *Canadian Film Reader*. Ed. Seth Feldman and Joyce Nelson. Toronto: Peter Martin Associates, 1977. 268-73.

Le Grice, Malcolm. "Current Developments." In *Abstract Film and Beyond*. Great Britain: Studio Vista, 1977.

Nelson, Joyce, comp. "David Rimmer: A Critical Collage." In *Canadian Film Reader*. Ed. Seth Feldman and Joyce Nelson. Toronto: Peter Martin Associates, 1977. 338-44.

Siegel, Lois. "Experimental Films, Ignored." Letter. *Cinema Canada* 41 (October 1977): 5.

Youngblood, Gene. "The New Canadian Cinema: Images from the Age of Paradox." In *Canadian Film Reader*. Ed. Seth Feldman and Joyce Nelson. Toronto: Peter Martin Associates, 1977. 323-32.

1978

Bassan, Raphael. "Experiences canadiennes." *Cinema Different* 21-22 (June 1978): 12-13.

Koller, George Csaba. "David Rimmer: Honesty of Vision." *Cinema Canada* 44 (February 1978): 18-21.

———. "Le cinéma expérimental." In *Les Cinémas canadiens.* Éd. Pierre Lherminier. Montréal: La Cinémathèque québécoise, 1978. 61-70.

Reif, Tony and Kirk Tougas. "Le Cinéma de la côte ouest." In *Les Cinémas canadiens*. Éd. Pierre Lherminier. Montréal: La Cinémathèque québécoise, 1978. 47-60.

Tomas, Albie. "The International Avant-Garde Film Festival: 1973." In *Polemics for a New Cinema.* Sydney: Wild and Woolley, 1978.

1979

Ward, Melinda. "Independent Film in Minneapolis/St. Paul." *Millennium Film Journal* 4-5 (Summer-Fall 1979): 144-52.

1980

Allen, Blaine. "David Rimmer's 'Surfacing on the Thames.'" *Cine-tracts* 9 3.1 (Winter 1980): 56-61.

Razutis, Al. "David Rimmer: A Critical Analysis." In *David Rimmer Film*. Exhibition Catalogue. Vancouver: Vancouver Art Gallery, 1980. n. pag.

1981

Browne, Colin. "David Rimmer: Re-Fusing the Contradictions." *Parachute* 22 (Spring 1981): 48-9.

Feldman, Seth. "Film: the Path Not Taken." *Canadian Forum*, LXI, 713 (November 1981): 39-40.

Lamb, Jamie. "'My Films Are Difficult to Watch.'" *Vancouver Sun* 8 January 1981: C1.

Nelson, Joyce. "Shorts—Al Neil: A Portrait." *Cinema Canada* 73 (April 1981): 47.

Perry, Art. "Entertainment: Rimmer Turns Films to Art." *Province* (Vancouver) 7 January 1981: A8.

1982

Elder, R. Bruce. "Redefining Experimental Film: Postmodern Practice in Canada." *Parachute* 27 (Summer 1982): 4-9.

———. "All Things in Their Times." *Cine-tracts* 5.1 (1982): 39-45.

Feldman, Seth. "Making It: Business as (Un)usual." *Cinema Canada* 81 (February 1982): 22-23.

Larouche, Michel. "Films experimentaux." *Parachute* 28 (September-October 1982): 36-37.

1983

"Artists' biographies: David Rimmer." In *Vancouver: Art and Artists 1931-1983*. Exhibition Catalogue. Vancouver: Vancouver Art Gallery, 1983. 422.

Elder, Bruce. "The Canadian Avant-Garde." In *Canadian Images: Festival of Canadian Film*. Festival Catalogue. Peterborough: Canadian Images, 1983. 27-29.

Razutis, Al. "Rediscovering Lost History: Avant-Garde Cinema 1960-69." In *Vancouver: Art and Artists 1931-1983*. Exhibition

Catalogue. Vancouver: Vancouver Art Gallery, 1983. 160-73.

———— and Tony Reif. "Critical Perspectives on Vancouver Avant-Garde Cinema 1970-83." In *Vancouver: Art and Artists 1931-1983*. Exhibition Catalogue. Vancouver: Vancouver Art Gallery, 1983. 286-299.

Wees, William C. "The Apparatus and the Avant-Garde." *Cinema Canada* 9 (June 1983), Special Supplement: 41-46.

1984

Banning, Kass. "Re/Vision: Reconsidering the British and Canadian Avant-Garde Cinemas." In *A Commonwealth*. Ed. Lori Keating and Kass Banning. Exhibition Catalogue. Toronto: Funnel, 1984. n. pag.

Elder, R. Bruce. "Image: Representations and Object: The Photographic Image in Canadian Avant-Garde Film." In *Take Two: A Tribute to Film in Canada*. Ed. Seth Feldman. Toronto: Irwin, 1984. 246-63.

————. "Experiments: The Photographic Image." In *Festival of Festivals, 1984*. Festival Catalogue. Toronto: Festival of Festivals, 1984. 156-64.

Morris, Peter. "Rimmer, David." In *The Film Companion*. Toronto: Irwin, 1984. 256-57.

————. "Surfacing on the Thames." In *The Film Companion*. Toronto: Irwin, 1984. 286.

Razutis, Al. "David Rimmer: A Critical Analysis." In *Take Two: A Tribute to Film in Canada*. Ed. Seth Feldman. Toronto: Irwin, 1984. 275-86.

———. "Ménage à Trois: Contemporary Film Theory, New Narrative and the Avant-Garde.' *OPSIS: The Canadian Journal of Avant-Garde and Political Cinema* 1.1 (Spring 1984): 52-66.

Testa, Bart. "Experimental Film: Its Past, Its Future." *Globe and Mail* (Toronto) 31 August 1984: E3.

1985

Bendahan, Raphaël. "Experimental Cinema in Canada." *Vanguard* 14, 5-6 (Summer 1985): 18-21.

1986

Elder, R. Bruce. "Experiments: the Photographic Image." *Northern Lights: A Programmers' Guide to the Festival of Festivals Retrospective*. Ed. Michael Sean Kiely. Ottawa: Canadian Film Institute, 1986. 87-103.

Everett-Green, Robert. "Frames from beyond the Fringe." *Globe and Mail* (Toronto), 13 May 1986: D9.

———. "Art: Celluloid Experiments." *Globe and Mail* (Toronto), 6 September 1986: C13.

Feyer, Ellen. "Cinema formansta: Suicidio artistico dell'avantguardia." In *New American Cinema: Il cinema indipendente Americano degli anni sessanta*, ed. Adriano Arpa.

Torino: Festival of Internazaionale Cinema Giovani, 1986. 147-52.

Russell, Katie. "Festival Hits Home." *NOW* (Toronto), 28 August-Sepember 1986: 23.

Sternberg, B. "On (Experimental) Film." *Cinema Canada* 128 (March 1986): 56.

―――. "On (Experimental) Film." *Cinema Canada* 130 (May 1986): 45.

1987

Allan, Blaine. "It's Not Finished Yet (Some Notes on Toronto Filmmaking)." In *Toronto: A Play of History*. Ed. Louise Dompierre. Exhibition Catalogue. Toronto: Power Plant, 1987. 83-92.

Clandfield, David. "Animated Film and Experimental Film." In *Canadian Film*. Toronto: Oxford University Press, 1987.

Insell, Maria. "En Garde: Echoes in the Museum of an Official Canadian Avant-Garde." *Speed* 1.1 (Spring 1987): 37-43.

Kerr, Richard. "On (Experimental) Film." *Cinema Canada* 145 (October 1987): 78-79.

"Montage of Voices." *Millennium Film Journal* 16-18 (Fall 1986-Winter 1987): 250-73.

Sternberg, B. "On (Experimental) Film." *Cinema Canada* 142 (June 1987): 48.

1988

Brakhage, Stan. "Some Words on the North." *American Book Review* 10.2 (May-June 1988): 5, 18.

Elder, R. Bruce. "Films, Experimental." In *Canadian Encyclopedia*. Ed. James H. Marsh. 2nd. ed. Edmonton: Hurtig, 1988.

———. "Rimmer, David." In *Canadian Encyclopedia*. Ed. James H. Marsh. 2nd ed. Edmonton: Hurtig, 1988.

Knight, Deborah. "Exquisite Nostalgia: Aesthetic Sensbility in the English-Canadian and Quebec Cinemas." *CineAction!* 11 (Winter 1987-1988): 30-37.

Merritt, Russell. "Review of *Film before Film (Was Geschach Wirklich Zwischen den Bildern?)* by Werner Nekes." *Film Quarterly* 41.1 (Autumn, 1987): 62-63.

1989

Elder, R. Bruce. "All Things in Their Time: Michael Snow's Back and Forth." In *Image and Identity: Reflections on Canadian Film and Culture*. Kitchener: Wilfrid Laurier University; Toronto: Academy of Canadian Cinema, 1989.

———. "The Photographic Image in Canadian Avant-Garde Film." In *Image and Identity: Reflections on Canadian Film and Culture*. Kitchener: Wilfrid Laurier University; Toronto: Academy of Canadian Cinema, 1989.

Falsetto, Mario. "Recent Films from Canada." in *International Experimental Film Congress*. Ed. Kathryn Elder et al. Exhibition Catalogue. Toronto: Art Gallery of Ontario, 1989. 68-70.

Insell, Maria. "En Garde: Desire in Ruins: Echoes in the Museum of an Official Canadian Avant-Garde." *Independent Eye* 10.3.

Russell, Catherine. "Reproduction and Repetition of History: David Rimmer's Found Footage." *CineAction!* 16 (Spring 1989): 52-58.

———. "Reviews: Film: Will the Reel Avant-Garde Please Stand Up?" *Fuse* 13.1-2 (fall 1989): 37-43.

Testa, Bart. "A Presence in the Landscape." In *Spirit in the Landscape*. Exhibition Catalogue. Toronto: Art Gallery of Ontario, 1989.

1990

Czernis, Loretta. "Pourquoi Est-Ce Que la Bête est Noire? A Brief Meditation on Canadian Experimental film." *Canadian Journal of Political and Social Theory* 14.1-14.3 (1990): 215-18.

Dorland, Michael. "'The Void is Not So Bleak': Rhetoric and Structure in Canadian Experimental Film." *Canadian Journal of Political and Social Theory* 14.1-14.3 (1990): 148-59.

Jonasson, Catherine, Ed. *New Experiments*. Exhibition Catalogue. Toronto: Art Gallery of Ontario, 1990.

1992

Allan, Blaine. "Handmade, or David Rimmer's Divine Mannequin." *Canadian Journal of Film Studies* 2.1 (1992): 63-80.

————. "David Rimmer's *Divine Mannequin.*" *Responses: In Honour of Peter Harcourt.* Ed. Blaine Allan et al. Kingston: Responsibility Press, 1992. 2-8.

Testa, Bart. "Early Episodes in the Career of the Gaze: Scanning the Primitive Tableau." In *Back and Forth: Early Cinema and the Avant-Garde.* Toronto: Art Gallery of Ontario, 1992.

1993

Bordwell, David and K. Thompson. "Mise-en-Scene in Space and Time." *Film Art: An Introduction*, 4th ed. New York: McGraw-Hill, 1993. 163-72.

David Rimmer: Films & Tapes 1967-1993. Exhibition Catalog. Toronto: Art Gallery of Ontario, 1993.

Russell, Catherine. "David Rimmer: Twilight in the Image Bank." *David Rimmer: Films & Tapes 1967-1993.* Exhibition Catalog. Toronto: Art Gallery of Ontario, 1993. 17-58.

1996

Falsetto, Mario. "Canadian catalogues and monographs of the avant-garde, 1989-1995 [Book Reviews]." *Cinémas: revue d'études cinématographique.* 7.1-2 (1996): 245-258.

Hoolboom, Mike. "As Seen on TV." *Vancouver: Representing the Postmodern City.* Ed. Paul Delany. Vancouver, BC: Arsenal Pulp Press, 1994.

2001

Fleer, Cornelia. "Alles im Fluss." *Film-dienst* 54.12 (June 2001): 37-39.

2002

Bears, William and White, Jerry, Eds. *North of Everything: English Canadian Cinema Since 1980.* Edmonton: University of Alberta Press, 2002.

2006

MacDonald, Scott. "Poetry and Film: Cinema as Publication." *Framework: The Journal of Cinema and Media* 47.2 (2006): 37-58.

Marks, Laura U. "The inhabited view: landscape in the films of David Rimmer." In *Landscape and Film*. Ed. Martin Lefebvre. New York : Routledge, 2006.

Mike Hoolboom (Essay) is a Canadian artist working in film and video. He is the author of three books: *Plague Years* (1998), *Fringe Film in Canada* (2000), and *Practical Dreamers* (2008). He is a founding member of the Pleasure Dome screening collective, and has worked as the artistic director of the Images Festival and the experimental film co-ordinator at Canadian Filmmakers Distribution Centre. He has won more than thirty international prizes, two lifetime achievement awards, and enjoyed nine international retrospectives of his work, most recently in Buenos Aires.

Alex MacKenzie (Interview) is a media artist working with light projection and expanded cinema. He was the founder and curator of The Edison Electric Gallery of Moving Images, The Blinding Light!! Cinema, and The Vancouver Underground Film Festival. His live media works are presented at festivals and underground screening spaces throughout Europe and North America, most recently at the Rotterdam International Film Festival and the K-raa-k Festival in Brussels. He is the co-editor of *Damp: Contemporary Vancouver Media Art* (Anvil Press, 2008), and is currently designing handmade film emulsions and manually-powered projection devices for installation and live performance.

Brian Ganter (Editor) is a writer, educator, and filmmaker. He is the Media Literacy Coordinator of the Pacific Cinémathèque's Education Department. Brian has published in a variety of journals, including *Textual Practice*, and has been an invited speaker and presenter at a variety of cinema studies and media studies conferences. In addition to a variety of short film and video works, Brian also wrote and directed the 2008 feature documentary *Metropole* which has screened internationally in festivals and forums in the U.S., Canada, and Europe. Brian is finishing his Ph.D. in cultural studies in the English Department at the University of Washington (Seattle) and teaches media and literary studies at Capilano University in Vancouver.

David Rimmer continues to produce new and exciting work in film and in other multimedia. Information about his films and upcoming screenings can be found at www.davidrimmerfilm.com.